FALL
BAKING

RDA ENTHUSIAST BRANDS, LLC
MILWAUKEE, WI

Taste of Home

EDITORIAL

Editor-in-Chief: Catherine Cassidy
Vice President, Content Operations: Kerri Balliet
Creative Director: Howard Greenberg

Managing Editor, Print & Digital Books: Mark Hagen
Associate Creative Director: Edwin Robles Jr.

Editor: Hazel Wheaton
Art Director: Raeann Thompson
Layout Designer: Nancy Novak
Editorial Services Manager: Dena Ahlers
Editorial Production Coordinator: Jill Banks
Copy Chief: Deb Warlaumont Mulvey
Copy Editors: Dulcie Shoener (senior), Ronald Kovach, Chris McLaughlin, Ellie Piper
Contributing Copy Editors: Michael Juley, Amy Rabideau Silvers
Editorial Services Administrator: Marie Brannon

Content Director: Julie Blume Benedict
Food Editors: Gina Nistico; James Schend; Peggy Woodward, RDN
Recipe Editors: Sue Ryon (lead), Irene Yeh

Culinary Director: Sarah Thompson
Test Cooks: Nicholas Iverson (lead), Matthew Hass
Food Stylists: Kathryn Conrad (lead), Lauren Knoelke, Shannon Roum
Prep Cooks: Bethany Van Jacobson (lead), Melissa Hansen, Aria C. Thornton
Culinary Team Assistant: Maria Petrella

Photography Director: Stephanie Marchese
Photographers: Dan Roberts, Jim Wieland
Photographer/Set Stylist: Grace Natoli Sheldon
Set Stylists: Melissa Franco (lead), Stacey Genaw, Dee Dee Schaefer
Set Stylist Assistant: Stephanie Chojnacki

Business Architect, Publishing Technologies: Amanda Harmatys
Business Analyst, Publishing Technologies: Kate Unger
Junior Business Analyst, Publishing Technologies: Shannon Stroud
Editorial Business Manager: Kristy Martin
Editorial Business Associate: Andrea Meiers

BUSINESS

Publisher: Donna Lindskog
Business Development Director, Taste of Home Live: Laurel Osman
Strategic Partnerships Manager, Taste of Home Live: Jamie Piette Andrzejewski

TRUSTED MEDIA BRANDS, INC.

President & Chief Executive Officer: Bonnie Kintzer
Chief Financial Officer: Dean Durbin
Chief Marketing Officer: C. Alec Casey
Chief Revenue Officer: Richard Sutton
Chief Digital Officer: Vince Errico
Senior Vice President, Global HR & Communications: Phyllis E. Gebhardt, SPHR; SHRM-SCP
General Counsel: Mark Sirota
Vice President, Product Marketing: Brian Kennedy
Vice President, Consumer Acquisition: Heather Plant
Vice President, Operations: Michael Garzone
Vice President, Consumer Marketing Planning: Jim Woods
Vice President, Digital Product & Technology: Nick Contardo
Vice President, Digital Content & Audience Development: Kari Hodes
Vice President, Financial Planning & Analysis: William Houston

For other *Taste of Home* books and products, visit us at *tasteofhome.com.*

International Standard Book Number: 978-1-61765-688-0
Library of Congress Control Number: 2017935169
Component Number: 118600013H

Cover Photographer: Jim Wieland
Set Stylist: Stacey Genaw
Food Stylist: Diane Armstrong

Pictured on front cover: Pumpkin Cheesecake, page 217
Pictured on back cover: Honey Bagels, page 20; Cherry Cheese Cupcakes, page 196
Pictured on title page: Cranberry Mocha Cheesecake, page 210
Pictured on spine: Cranberry Lemon Sandwiches, page 80

Printed in China.
1 3 5 7 9 10 8 6 4 2

GRAHAM STREUSEL COFFEE CAKE, 15

YUMMY APRICOT PECAN BREAD, 38

WALNUT-FILLED PILLOWS, 99

MOIST LEMON CHIFFON CAKE, 192

CONTENTS

GET SOCIAL WITH US

LIKE US
facebook.com/tasteofhome

TWEET US
twitter.com/tasteofhome

FOLLOW US
@ tasteofhome

PIN US
pinterest.com/taste_of_home

SHOP WITH US
shoptasteofhome.com

SHARE A RECIPE
tasteofhome.com/submit

CRANBERRY CHEESE
CRUMB PIE, 152

Celebrate the
Flavors of Fall!

Apples. Pumpkin. Pecan. Cranberry. Maple. The sweet, rich flavors of the harvest are perfect for creating the ultimate in homemade comfort—baked goods! Whether it's a basket of muffins, a fruit pie with a pastry crust, a plate full of cookies or a loaf of homemade bread, nothing sets mouths watering like the tantalizing aroma of a treat fresh from the oven.

Tap into the incredible variety of fall flavors to make goodies to share with your friends and family. Quick breads, rolls, brownies and bars, cobblers and crisps, decadent cheesecakes...whether you're baking in a 9x13 pan, muffin tins or a cast-iron skillet, the choices are endless. A special chapter offers a collection of twists on traditional baked treats,

GINGER-LIME
PEAR COBBLER, 174

GARLIC HERB
BUBBLE LOAF, 71

with bread puddings, pretzels, popovers...all outside-the-box options that don't come from a box! **Taste of Home Fall Baking** presents 113 favorite recipes from home cooks like you that celebrate the best of the turning of the season.

This delightful collection of recipes makes it easy to create freshly baked delicacies that will make your kitchen smell like heaven—and your family eager for a taste. All of the recipes were tested in the *Taste of Home Test Kitchen,* so you know they'll turn out just right.

GINGER PLUM
TART 132

Pecan Coffee Cake, p. 24

CHAPTER 1

MORNING BITES

The perfect pairing for morning coffee is a fresh-baked treat!

Almond Streusel Rolls

I've used these sweet rolls as a deliciously different dessert, too. Often, they aren't even cool before the pan is empty!

—**PERLENE HOEKEMA** LYNDEN, WA

PREP: 40 MIN. + RISING
BAKE: 35 MIN. + COOLING
MAKES: 1 DOZEN

- 2 packages (¼ ounce each) active dry yeast
- ¾ cup warm water (110° to 115°)
- ¾ cup warm milk (110° to 115°)
- ¼ cup butter, softened
- ½ cup sugar
- 2 large eggs
- 1 teaspoon salt
- 5¼ to 5½ cups all-purpose flour

FILLING
- ½ cup almond paste
- ¼ cup butter, softened
- ½ cup packed brown sugar
- ¼ teaspoon almond extract

TOPPING
- 3 tablespoons sugar
- 1 tablespoon all-purpose flour
- 1 tablespoon butter

ICING
- 1½ cups confectioners' sugar
- ¼ teaspoon almond extract
- 1 to 2 tablespoons milk

1. In a large bowl, dissolve yeast in warm water. Add milk, butter, sugar, eggs, salt and 2 cups of the flour. Beat until smooth. Stir in enough remaining flour to form a soft dough.

2. Turn onto a floured surface; knead until smooth and elastic, about 6-8 minutes. Place in a greased bowl, turning once to grease top. Cover and let rise in a warm place until doubled, about 1 hour.

3. Punch the dough down; roll out to a 15x10-in. rectangle. In a large bowl, beat filling ingredients until smooth. Spread over dough.

4. Roll up jelly-roll style, starting with a short side; seal seams. Cut into 12 slices. Place in a greased 13x9-in. baking pan or 12-in. ovenproof skillet. Cover and let rise in a warm place until doubled, about 30 minutes.

5. Combine topping ingredients; sprinkle over the rolls. Bake at 350° for 35-40 minutes or until golden brown. Cool on a wire rack.

6. In a small bowl, mix confectioners' sugar, extract and enough milk to achieve drizzling consistency; drizzle over rolls.

NUTRITION FACTS 1 roll: 482 cal., 13g fat (6g sat. fat), 61mg chol., 308mg sod., 83g carb. (37g sugars, 2g fiber), 8g pro.

Overnight Cherry Danish

These rolls, with their cherry-filled centers, melt in your mouth and store well, unfrosted, in the freezer.
—LEANN SAUDER TREMONT, IL

PREP: 1½ HOURS + CHILLING
BAKE: 15 MIN. + COOLING
MAKES: 3 DOZEN

- 2 packages (¼ ounce each) active dry yeast
- ½ cup warm 2% milk (110° to 115°)
- 6 cups all-purpose flour
- ⅓ cup sugar
- 2 teaspoons salt
- 1 cup cold butter, cubed
- 1½ cups warm half-and-half cream (70° to 80°)
- 6 large egg yolks
- 1 can (21 ounces) cherry pie filling

ICING
- 3 cups confectioners' sugar
- 2 tablespoons butter, softened
- ¼ teaspoon vanilla extract
  Dash salt
- 4 to 5 tablespoons half-and-half cream

1. In a small bowl, dissolve yeast in warm milk. In a large bowl, combine flour, sugar and salt. Cut in butter until crumbly. Add the yeast mixture, cream and egg yolks; stir until the mixture forms a soft dough (dough will be sticky). Refrigerate, covered, overnight.

2. Punch down the dough. Turn onto a lightly floured surface; divide into four portions. Roll each portion into an 18x4-in. rectangle; cut each rectangle into 4x1-in. strips.

3. Place two strips side by side; twist together. Shape into a ring and pinch the ends together. Repeat with the remaining strips. Place 2 in. apart on greased baking sheets. Cover with kitchen towels; let rise in a warm place until doubled, about 45 minutes.

4. Preheat oven to 350°. Using the end of a wooden spoon handle, make a ½-in.-deep indentation in the center of each pastry. Fill each with about 1 tablespoon pie filling. Bake 14-16 minutes or until lightly browned. Remove from pans to wire racks to cool.

5. For icing, in a bowl, beat confectioners' sugar, butter, vanilla, salt and enough cream to reach the desired consistency. Drizzle over the pastry.

NUTRITION FACTS 1 pastry: 218 cal., 8g fat (5g sat. fat), 55mg chol., 188mg sodium, 33g carb. (16g sugars, 1g fiber), 3g pro.

Swedish Puff Coffee Cake

Some of my most treasured childhood memories involve waking up to the heavenly scent of this almond-glazed coffee cake baking in the oven.

—MARY SHENK DEKALB, IL

PREP: 35 MIN. • **BAKE:** 30 MIN. + COOLING
MAKES: 12 SERVINGS

- 1 cup all-purpose flour
- ½ cup cold butter, cubed
- 2 tablespoons ice water

TOPPING

- 1 cup water
- ½ cup butter
- 1 teaspoon almond extract
- 1 cup all-purpose flour
- 3 large eggs

GLAZE

- 1 cup confectioners' sugar
- 2 tablespoons butter, softened
- 1 tablespoon 2% milk
- 1 teaspoon almond extract
- 1 cup flaked coconut

1. Preheat oven to 375°. Place flour in a small bowl; cut in butter until crumbly. Gradually add ice water, tossing with a fork until dough holds together when pressed. On an ungreased baking sheet, press the dough into a 10-in. circle.

2. For topping, in a large saucepan, bring water and butter to a rolling boil. Remove from heat; stir in extract. Add the flour all at once and beat until blended. Cook over medium heat, stirring vigorously, until the mixture pulls away from sides of pan and forms a ball. Remove from heat; let stand for 5 minutes.

3. Add eggs, one at a time, beating until smooth after each addition. Continue beating until the mixture is smooth and shiny; spread over the pastry dough.

4. Bake 30-35 minutes or until lightly browned. Cover loosely with foil during the last 5 minutes if needed to prevent overbrowning. Remove from pan to a wire rack to cool completely.

5. For glaze, in a small bowl, beat the confectioners' sugar, butter, milk and extract until smooth. Spread over top; sprinkle with coconut.

NUTRITION FACTS 1 slice: 326 cal., 21g fat (14g sat. fat), 98mg chol., 160mg sod., 30g carb. (12g sugars, 1g fiber), 4g pro.

Graham Streusel Coffee Cake

I make this sweet coffee cake often; it's so quick and easy, it looks beautiful and it tastes even better!

—BLANCHE WHYTSELL ARNOLDSBURG, WV

PREP: 20 MIN. • **BAKE:** 40 MIN. + COOLING
MAKES: 16 SERVINGS

1½ cups graham cracker crumbs
¾ cup packed brown sugar
¾ cup chopped pecans
1½ teaspoons ground cinnamon
⅔ cup butter, melted
1 package yellow cake mix (regular size)
½ cup confectioners' sugar
1 tablespoon milk

1. In a small bowl, combine cracker crumbs, brown sugar, pecans and cinnamon. Stir in butter; set aside. Prepare cake mix according to the package directions.

2. Pour half of the batter into a greased 13x9-in. baking pan. Sprinkle with half of the graham cracker mixture. Carefully spoon the remaining batter on top. Sprinkle with the remaining graham cracker mixture.

3. Bake at 350° for 40-45 minutes or until a toothpick inserted in the center comes out clean. Cool on a wire rack. Combine confectioners' sugar and milk; drizzle over the coffee cake.

NUTRITION FACTS 1 piece: 329 cal., 15g fat (6g sat. fat), 21mg chol., 332mg sod., 46g carb. (30g sugars, 2g fiber), 3g pro.

TOP TIP

Many factors affect baking times, so they are never exact. To avoid burning your cake, check for doneness 10-15 minutes before the end of the recommended baking time. If the cake is not done, test it again in few more minutes.

Cinnamon Coffee Cake

I love the excellent texture of this old-fashioned coffee cake topped and filled with streusel. Always a crowd-pleaser, its lovely vanilla flavor enriched with sour cream may remind you of brunch at Grandma's!
—**ELEANOR HARRIS** CAPE CORAL, FL

PREP: 20 MIN. • **BAKE:** 1 HOUR + COOLING
MAKES: 20 SERVINGS

1	cup butter, softened
2¾	cups sugar, divided
4	large eggs
2	teaspoons vanilla extract
3	cups all-purpose flour
1	teaspoon baking soda
1	teaspoon salt
2	cups sour cream
2	tablespoons ground cinnamon
½	cup chopped walnuts

1. In a large bowl, cream butter and 2 cups of sugar until light and fluffy. Add eggs, one at a time, beating well after each addition. Beat in vanilla. Combine flour, baking soda and salt; add alternately with sour cream, beating just enough after each addition to keep the batter smooth.

2. Spoon a third of the batter into a greased 10-in. tube pan. Combine cinnamon, nuts and the remaining sugar; sprinkle a third over the batter in the pan. Repeat layers two more times. Bake at 350° for 60-65 minutes or until a toothpick inserted in the center comes out clean. Cool coffee cake in the pan for 15 minutes before removing from pan to a wire rack to cool completely.

NUTRITION FACTS 1 piece: 340 cal., 16g fat (9g sat. fat), 83mg chol., 299mg sod., 44g carb. (28g sugars, 1g fiber), 5g pro.

Kate Smith Coffee Cake

When I lived in an orphanage over 50 years ago, I helped out in the kitchen and often made this wonderful coffee cake, dutifully following the recipe in the cookbook they used. Years later, seeing Kate Smith on television, I was delighted to realize I had been using a favorite recipe from her cookbook!

—RUTH NAST WATERFORD, CT

PREP: 15 MIN. • **BAKE:** 20 MIN.
MAKES: 6 SERVINGS

1 large egg
¼ cup butter, melted
⅓ cup milk
1 cup all-purpose flour
¼ cup sugar
2 teaspoons baking powder
¼ teaspoon salt
1 cup bran flakes, crushed

TOPPING
2 teaspoons butter, softened
2 tablespoons brown sugar
⅓ cup bran flakes, crushed

In a bowl, combine egg, butter and milk. In a second bowl, combine flour, sugar, baking powder and salt; stir into the batter. Add bran flakes. Spread into a greased 8-in. round baking pan or 8-in. ovenproof skillet. Combine topping ingredients; sprinkle over the batter. Bake at 375° for 18-22 minutes or until a toothpick inserted in the center comes out clean. Serve warm.

NUTRITION FACTS 1 slice: 253 cal., 11g fat (6g sat. fat), 61mg chol., 406mg sod., 37g carb. (15g sugars, 2g fiber), 5g pro.

Honey Bagels

Who has time to make from-scratch bagels? You do, with this easy recipe! The chewy golden bagels offer a hint of honey and are sure to impress the pickiest of palates.
—*TASTE OF HOME* **TEST KITCHEN**

PREP: 1 HOUR + STANDING
BAKE: 20 MIN.
MAKES: 1 DOZEN

- 1 tablespoon active dry yeast
- 1¼ cups warm water (110° to 115°)
- 3 tablespoons canola oil
- 3 tablespoons sugar
- 3 tablespoons plus ¼ cup honey, divided
- 1 teaspoon brown sugar
- 1½ teaspoons salt
- 1 large egg
- 4 to 5 cups bread flour
- 1 tablespoon dried minced onion
- 1 tablespoon sesame seeds
- 1 tablespoon poppy seeds

1. In a large bowl, dissolve yeast in warm water. Add oil, sugar, 3 tablespoons of the honey, brown sugar, salt and egg; mix well. Stir in enough flour to form a soft dough.

2. Turn out onto a floured surface; knead until a smooth, firm dough forms, about 8-10 minutes. Cover and let rest for 10 minutes.

3. Punch the dough down. Shape into 12 balls. Push your thumb through the center of each ball to form a 1½-in. hole. Stretch and shape dough to form an even ring. Place on a floured surface. Cover and let rest for 10 minutes; flatten bagels slightly.

4. In a large saucepan or Dutch oven, bring 8 cups water and the remaining honey to a boil. Drop the bagels, one at a time, into boiling water. Cook for 45 seconds; turn and cook 45 seconds longer. Remove the bagels with a slotted spoon; drain and sprinkle with onion, sesame and poppy seeds.

5. Place the bagels 2 in. apart on baking sheets lined with parchment paper. Bake at 425° for 12 minutes. Turn and bake 5 minutes longer or until golden brown.

NUTRITION FACTS 1 bagel: 265 cal., 5g fat (1g sat. fat), 16mg chol., 303mg sod., 48g carb. (14g sugars, 2g fiber), 7g pro.

Cranberry-Pear Coffee Cake

This is my favorite coffee cake to make for last-minute occasions. I also make it to give to friends, because it always turns out just right.
—**BEVERLY LOVEGROVE** WINNIPEG, MB

PREP: 25 MIN. • **BAKE:** 40 MIN. + COOLING
MAKES: 12 SERVINGS

2	cups all-purpose flour
¾	cup plus 1 tablespoon sugar, divided
1½	teaspoons ground cinnamon
1	teaspoon baking powder
½	teaspoon salt
¼	teaspoon baking soda
1	large egg
¾	cup buttermilk
¼	cup butter, melted
1	teaspoon vanilla extract
1	large pear, peeled and coarsely chopped
1	cup fresh or frozen cranberries, thawed and chopped
1	teaspoon grated orange peel
1	tablespoon brown sugar

1. In a large bowl, combine flour, ¾ cup of the sugar, cinnamon, baking powder, salt and baking soda. In a small bowl, whisk egg, buttermilk, butter and vanilla. Stir into the dry ingredients just until moistened. Fold in pear, cranberries and orange peel.

2. Transfer to a 9-in. springform pan coated with cooking spray and dusted with flour. Combine brown sugar and remaining sugar; sprinkle over the batter. Bake at 350° for 40-45 minutes or until a toothpick inserted in the center comes out clean. Cool in the pan for 10 minutes before removing to a wire rack. Serve warm.

NUTRITION FACTS 1 slice: 194 cal., 5g fat (3g sat. fat), 29mg chol., 219mg sod., 35g carb. (18g sugars, 1g fiber), 3g pro. *Diabetic Exchanges:* 2 starch, 1 fat.

Pecan Coffee Cake

My mom serves this nutty coffee cake for Christmas breakfast each year. The simple recipe is a big time-saver on such a busy morning, and everyone loves the crunchy pecan topping.

—BECKY WAX TUSCOLA, IL

PREP: 15 MIN. • **BAKE:** 30 MIN.
MAKES: 15 SERVINGS

- 1 package yellow cake mix (regular size)
- 1 package (3.4 ounces) instant vanilla pudding mix
- 1 cup sour cream
- 4 large eggs
- 1/3 cup canola oil
- 2 teaspoons vanilla extract
- 2/3 cup chopped pecans
- 1/3 cup sugar
- 2 teaspoons ground cinnamon
- 1/2 cup confectioners' sugar
- 2 tablespoons orange juice

1. In a large bowl, combine the first six ingredients; beat on low for 30 seconds. Beat on medium for 2 minutes. Pour into a greased 13x9-in. baking pan. Combine pecans, sugar and cinnamon; sprinkle over the batter. Cut through the batter with a knife to swirl the pecan mixture.

2. Bake at 350° for 30-35 minutes or until a toothpick inserted in the center comes out clean.

3. Meanwhile, in a small bowl, combine confectioners' sugar and orange juice until smooth; drizzle over warm coffee cake. Cool on a wire rack.

NUTRITION FACTS 1 piece: 335 cal., 16g fat (4g sat. fat), 67mg chol., 332mg sod., 44g carb. (29g sugars, 1g fiber), 4g pro.

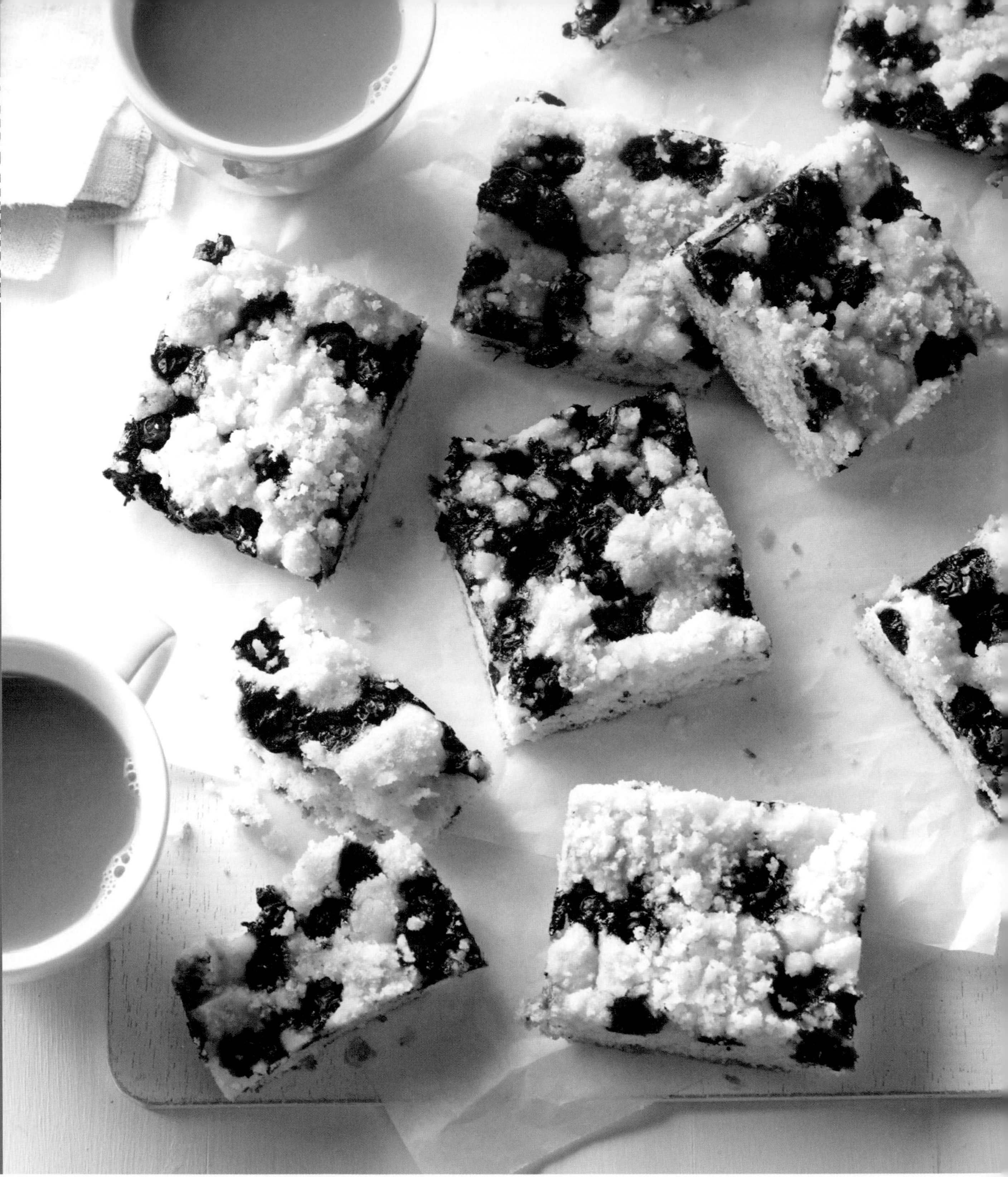

Blueberry Kuchen

I freeze the beautiful, plump blueberries that we get in the summer to have them available to make this delicious coffee cake all year round.

—**ANNE KRUEGER** RICHMOND, BC

PREP: 10 MIN. • **BAKE:** 40 MIN.
MAKES: 12 SERVINGS

1½ cups all-purpose flour
¾ cup sugar
2 teaspoons baking powder
1½ teaspoons grated lemon peel
½ teaspoon ground nutmeg
¼ teaspoon salt
⅔ cup milk
¼ cup butter, melted
1 large egg, beaten
1 teaspoon vanilla extract
2 cups fresh or frozen blueberries

TOPPING
¾ cup sugar
½ cup all-purpose flour
¼ cup butter, melted

1. In a bowl, combine the first six ingredients. Add milk, butter, egg and vanilla. Beat for 2 minutes or until the mixture is well blended.

2. Pour into a greased 13x9-in. baking dish. Sprinkle with blueberries. In a bowl, combine sugar and flour; add butter. Toss with a fork until crumbly; sprinkle over the blueberries. Bake at 350° for 40 minutes or until cake is lightly browned.

NUTRITION FACTS 1 piece: 271 cal., 9g fat (5g sat. fat), 37mg chol., 189mg sod., 45g carb. (28g sugars, 1g fiber), 3g pro.

> **DID YOU KNOW?**
>
> In 2000, South Dakota officially designated kuchen its official state dessert. Kuchen is the German word for "cake," and it can describe any of a variety of sweet desserts and pastries.

Yummy Apricot Pecan Bread, p. 38

CHAPTER 2

QUICK BREADS
Tasty bread, scones, muffins and biscuits—they all come together fast!

Rustic Oatmeal Scones

My family loves scones, but traditional recipes contain excessive fat and calories. After lots of experimentation, I came up with this alternative recipe. The delicious flavor, amazing texture and nutrient density are well worth the effort.

—GAIL D'URSO CARLISLE, PA

PREP: 20 MIN. • **BAKE:** 15 MIN.
MAKES: 16 SCONES

1½ cups all-purpose flour
½ cup whole wheat flour
½ cup sugar
2 teaspoons baking powder
1 teaspoon baking soda
¾ teaspoon salt
¼ cup cold butter, cubed
2 cups quick-cooking oats
1 cup dried blueberries or raisins
1 cup plain yogurt
3 tablespoons fat-free milk, divided
  Coarse sugar

1. Preheat oven to 400°. In a large bowl, whisk the first six ingredients. Cut in butter until mixture resembles coarse crumbs. Stir in oats and blueberries. In another bowl, whisk yogurt and 1 tablespoon of the milk until blended; stir into the crumb mixture just until moistened.

2. Turn onto a lightly floured surface; knead gently 10 times. Divide dough in half; pat each half into a 7-in. circle. Cut each circle into eight wedges. Place the wedges on a baking sheet coated with cooking spray. Brush the tops with the remaining milk. Sprinkle with coarse sugar.

3. Bake for 13-15 minutes or until golden brown. Serve warm.

NUTRITION FACTS 1 scone (calculated without coarse sugar): 186 cal., 4g fat (2g sat. fat), 11mg chol., 273mg sod., 32g carb. (11g sugars, 3g fiber), 4g pro. *Diabetic Exchanges:* 2 starch, 1 fat.

Java Muffins

I look to these muffins to get me going in the morning. They're especially satisfying with a cup of coffee!

—ZAINAB AHMED MOUNTLAKE TERRACE, WA

START TO FINISH: 30 MIN.
MAKES: 1 DOZEN

¼ cup butter, softened
1 cup packed brown sugar
2 large eggs
¼ cup unsweetened applesauce
½ cup buttermilk
½ cup strong brewed coffee
1 tablespoon instant coffee granules
½ teaspoon vanilla extract
1 cup all-purpose flour
¾ cup whole wheat flour
1½ teaspoons baking powder
½ teaspoon baking soda
½ teaspoon ground cinnamon
¼ teaspoon salt
½ cup finely chopped pecans, divided

1. Preheat oven to 375°. In a large bowl, beat the butter and brown sugar until crumbly, about 2 minutes. Add eggs; mix well. Beat in applesauce. In a small bowl, whisk buttermilk, coffee, coffee granules and vanilla until granules are dissolved; gradually add to the butter mixture.

2. In another bowl, whisk flours, baking powder, baking soda, cinnamon and salt. Add to the butter mixture; stir just until moistened. Fold in ¼ cup of the pecans.

3. Coat 12 muffin cups with cooking spray or use paper liners; fill each cup three-fourths full. Sprinkle with the remaining pecans. Bake 15-20 minutes or until a toothpick inserted in the center of a muffin comes out clean. Cool in pan for 5 minutes before removing muffins from pan to a wire rack. Serve warm.

NUTRITION FACTS 1 muffin: 220 cal., 9g fat (3g sat. fat), 46mg chol., 209mg sod., 33g carb. (19g sugars, 2g fiber), 4g pro. *Diabetic Exchanges:* 2 starch, 1½ fat.

Hurry-Up Biscuits

When I was young, my mom would make these biscuits with fresh cream she got from a local farmer. I don't go to those lengths anymore, but the family recipe is still a real treat.
—**BEVERLY SPRAGUE** BALTIMORE, MD

START TO FINISH: 30 MIN.
MAKES: 1 DOZEN

3   cups all-purpose flour
4   teaspoons baking powder
4   teaspoons sugar
1   teaspoon salt
2   cups heavy whipping cream

1. Preheat oven to 375°. In a large bowl, whisk flour, baking powder, sugar and salt. Add cream; stir just until moistened.

2. Drop by ¼ cupfuls 1 in. apart onto greased baking sheets. Bake 17-20 minutes or until bottoms are golden brown. Serve warm.

NUTRITION FACTS 1 biscuit: 256 cal. 15g fat (9g sat. fat), 54mg chol., 346mg sod., 26g carb. (2g sugars, 1g fiber), 4g pro.

HOW TO

TEST BAKING POWDER FOR FRESHNESS

If you're not sure your baking powder is fresh, here's how to test it: Place 1 teaspoon baking powder in a cup and add ⅓ cup hot tap water. If active bubbling occurs, the powder is fine to use.

Chocolate Chip-Cranberry Scones

My daughter started making these as a healthier alternative to cookies for our cookie-loving family. For a more citrusy flavor, use orange-flavored cranberries.

—NICHOLE JONES IDAHO FALLS, ID

START TO FINISH: 30 MIN.
MAKES: 1 DOZEN

---

   2   cups all-purpose flour
   3   tablespoons brown sugar
   2   teaspoons baking powder
   1   teaspoon grated orange peel
   $1/2$ teaspoon salt
   $1/2$ teaspoon baking soda
   $1/4$ cup cold butter
   1   cup plain yogurt
   1   large egg yolk
   $1/2$ cup dried cranberries
   $1/2$ cup semisweet chocolate chips

1. Preheat oven to 400°. In a large bowl, whisk the first six ingredients. Cut in butter until mixture resembles coarse crumbs. In another bowl, whisk yogurt and egg yolk; stir into the crumb mixture just until moistened. Stir in cranberries and chocolate chips.

2. Turn onto a floured surface; knead gently 10 times. Pat dough into an 8-in. circle. Cut into 12 wedges. Place wedges on a baking sheet coated with cooking spray. Bake 10-12 minutes or until golden brown. Serve warm.

FREEZE OPTION Freeze cooled scones in resealable plastic freezer bags. To use, thaw at room temperature or, if desired, microwave each scone on high for 20-30 seconds or until heated through.

NUTRITION FACTS 1 scone: 189 cal., 7g fat (4g sat. fat), 28mg chol., 264mg sod., 29g carb. (11g sugars, 1g fiber), 3g pro. *Diabetic Exchanges:* 2 starch, 1 fat.

Yummy Apricot Pecan Bread

Every time I prepare this bread, I receive raves. It's perfect with coffee or as a gift, plus it's really quick and easy to prepare.

—JOAN HALLFORD NORTH RICHLAND HILLS, TX

PREP: 20 MIN. • **BAKE:** 40 MIN.
MAKES: 2 LOAVES (12 SLICES EACH)

2½ cups all-purpose flour
¾ cup sugar
 2 teaspoons baking soda
 1 teaspoon ground cinnamon
¼ teaspoon salt
¼ teaspoon ground nutmeg
 1 cup 2% milk
 2 large eggs
⅓ cup butter, melted
 2 cups shredded cheddar cheese
 1 cup finely chopped dried apricots
¾ cup finely chopped pecans

TOPPING
 3 tablespoons packed brown sugar
 1 tablespoon butter
½ teaspoon ground cinnamon

1. Preheat oven to 350°. In a large bowl, combine the first six ingredients. In a small bowl, beat milk, eggs and butter; stir into the dry ingredients just until moistened. Fold in cheese, apricots and pecans. Spoon into two greased 8x4-in. loaf pans. Combine the topping ingredients; sprinkle over the batter.

2. Bake for 40-45 minutes or until a toothpick inserted in the center comes out clean. Cool in pans for 10 minutes before removing from pans to wire racks.

FREEZE OPTION Securely wrap and freeze cooled loaves in plastic wrap and foil. To use, thaw at room temperature.

NUTRITION FACTS 1 slice: 189 cal., 9g fat (4g sat. fat), 36mg chol., 223mg sod., 23g carb. (11g sugars, 1g fiber), 5g pro.

DID YOU KNOW?

Most quick breads should be baked shortly after dry ingredients and liquid ingredients are combined because the leaveners begin producing gas once they are moistened. If allowed to stand too long before baking, the bread may have a sunken center.

Apple & Cheddar Mini Scones

Cheese and sage go well with apples, so why not put them all together in scones? These mini bites make a fall brunch, tailgate or party even more fun.

—**SUE GRONHOLZ** BEAVER DAM, WI

PREP: 25 MIN. • **BAKE:** 10 MIN.
MAKES: 32 SCONES

- 3 cups all-purpose flour
- 3 teaspoons baking powder
- ½ teaspoon salt
- ½ teaspoon baking soda
- 1 cup cold butter, cubed
- 1 large egg
- ¾ cup vanilla yogurt
- 3 tablespoons 2% milk, divided
- ⅓ cup shredded peeled apple
- ⅓ cup shredded sharp cheddar cheese
- 1 tablespoon minced fresh sage
- 1 tablespoon sugar

1. Preheat oven to 425°. In a large bowl, whisk flour, baking powder, salt and baking soda. Cut in butter until the mixture resembles coarse crumbs. In another bowl, whisk egg, yogurt and 2 tablespoons of the milk; stir into the crumb mixture just until moistened. Stir in apple, cheese and sage.

2. Turn onto a lightly floured surface; knead gently 10 times. Divide dough in half; pat each half into a 6-in. circle. Cut each circle into eight wedges; cut each wedge in half.

3. Transfer to parchment paper-lined baking sheets. Brush tops with the remaining milk; sprinkle with sugar. Bake 10-12 minutes or until golden brown. Serve warm.

NUTRITION FACTS 1 mini scone: 109 cal., 7g fat (4g sat. fat), 23mg chol., 159mg sod., 10g carb.(2g sugars, 0 fiber), 2g pro.

A Bit Nutty Boston Brown Bread

Hearty and dense, my homemade Boston brown bread features hazelnuts for a delightfully nutty taste. Thick slices go well with just about anything, from soups and stews to roasts and casseroles.

—LORRAINE CALAND SHUNIAH, ON

PREP: 30 MIN. • **BAKE:** 45 MIN. + COOLING
MAKES: 2 LOAVES (12 SLICES EACH)

- 3 cups whole wheat flour
- 1 cup all-purpose flour
- 2½ teaspoons baking soda
- 1 teaspoon salt
- 2½ cups buttermilk
- 1 cup molasses
- 1 cup golden raisins
- ¾ cup chopped hazelnuts

1. Preheat oven to 350°. In a large bowl, combine the flours, baking soda and salt. In a small bowl, whisk buttermilk and molasses. Stir into the dry ingredients just until moistened. Fold in raisins and nuts. Transfer to two greased 8x4-in. loaf pans.

2. Bake for 45-50 minutes or until a toothpick inserted in the center comes out clean. Cool in pans for 10 minutes before removing from pans to wire racks.

NOTE To toast nuts, bake in a shallow pan in a 350° oven for 5-10 minutes or cook in a skillet over low heat until lightly browned, stirring occasionally.

NUTRITION FACTS 1 slice: 159 cal., 3g fat (0 sat. fat), 1mg chol., 263mg sod., 31g carb. (13g sugars, 3g fiber), 4g pro.

Jumbo Caramel Banana Muffins

Love banana bread? These flavorful muffins, drizzled with sweet caramel icing, will fit the bill in a big way.

—KATHERINE MCCLELLAND DEEP BROOK, NS

PREP: 20 MIN. • **BAKE:** 25 MIN. + COOLING
MAKES: 6 MUFFINS

¼ cup shortening
1 cup sugar
1 large egg
1½ cups mashed ripe bananas (about 3 large)
1 teaspoon vanilla extract
1½ cups all-purpose flour
1 teaspoon baking soda
¼ teaspoon salt

CARAMEL ICING
2 tablespoons butter
¼ cup packed brown sugar
1 tablespoon 2% milk
½ cup confectioners' sugar

1. Preheat oven to 350°. In a large bowl, cream shortening and sugar until light and fluffy. Beat in egg. Beat in bananas and vanilla. Combine flour, baking soda and salt; add to the creamed mixture just until moistened.

2. Fill paper-lined jumbo muffin cups three-fourths full. Bake for 23-28 minutes or until a toothpick inserted in the center of a muffin comes out clean. Cool in pan for 5 minutes before removing from pan to a wire rack to cool completely.

3. For icing, in a small saucepan, melt butter over medium heat. Stir in brown sugar and milk; bring to a boil. Cool slightly. Beat in confectioners' sugar until smooth. Transfer to a small resealable plastic bag; cut a small hole in a corner of the bag and drizzle icing over the muffins.

NUTRITION FACTS 1 muffin: 490 cal., 13g fat (5g sat. fat), 46mg chol., 364mg sod., 89g carb. (62g sugars, 2g fiber), 5g pro.

English Marmalade Pecan Bread

My dad was Canadian but had a very British upbringing. And, boy, did he love his marmalade! Because it can be an acquired taste, I baked the jam into this nutty bread. Everyone loved it—even my kids.
—**NANCY HEISHMAN** LAS VEGAS, NV

PREP: 20 MIN. • **BAKE:** 50 MIN. + COOLING
MAKES: 1 LOAF (16 SLICES)

- ½ cup butter, softened
- ½ cup packed brown sugar
- 2 large eggs
- 1 jar (10 ounces) orange marmalade spreadable fruit
- 2⅔ cups all-purpose flour
- 3 teaspoons baking powder
- 2 teaspoons ground cinnamon
- 1 teaspoon salt
- ⅓ cup orange juice
- ½ cup chopped pecans

1. Preheat oven to 350°. Grease and flour a 9x5-in. loaf pan. In a large bowl, beat butter and brown sugar until blended. Add eggs, one at a time, beating well after each addition. Gradually beat in marmalade. In another bowl, whisk flour, baking powder, cinnamon and salt; add to the butter mixture alternately with orange juice, beating well after each addition. Fold in pecans.

2. Transfer to prepared pan. Bake 50-60 minutes or until a toothpick inserted in center comes out clean. Cool in pan 10 minutes before removing to a wire rack to cool.

FREEZE OPTION Securely wrap cooled loaf in plastic wrap and foil to freeze. To use, thaw wrapped loaf at room temperature. If desired, warm slices in toaster or microwave.

NUTRITION FACTS 1 slice: 226 cal., 9g fat (4g sat. fat), 39mg chol., 132mg sod., 33g carb. (15g sugars, 1g fiber), 3g pro.

Flaky Whole Wheat Biscuits

Whole wheat flour gives these biscuits a nutty flavor. Ever since I started making these, white flour biscuits just don't taste as good! Pair them with soup or slather them with whipped cream and sweetened berries for a dessert treat.
—**TRISHA KRUSE** EAGLE, ID

START TO FINISH: 25 MIN.
MAKES: 10 BISCUITS

1	cup all-purpose flour
1	cup whole wheat flour
3	teaspoons baking powder
1	tablespoon brown sugar
1	teaspoon baking soda
½	teaspoon salt
¼	cup cold butter
1	cup 2% milk

1. Preheat oven to 425°. In a large bowl, combine the first six ingredients. Cut in butter until the mixture resembles coarse crumbs. Stir in milk just until moistened. Turn onto a lightly floured surface; knead 8-10 times.

2. Pat or roll out dough to ½-in. thickness; cut with a floured 2½-in. biscuit cutter. Place 2 in. apart on an ungreased baking sheet. Bake for 8-10 minutes or until golden brown.

NUTRITION FACTS 1 biscuit: 144 cal., 6g fat (3g sat. fat), 14mg chol., 417mg sod., 21g carb. (3g sugars, 2g fiber), 4g pro. *Diabetic Exchanges:* 1½ starch, 1 fat.

Cream Cheese Cranberry Muffins

Moist and packed with colorful berries, these marvelous muffins are a seasonal specialty. They are light and tasty, and they freeze very well.

—LEONARD KESZLER BISMARCK, ND

PREP: 15 MIN. • **BAKE:** 20 MIN.
MAKES: 2 DOZEN

1 cup butter, softened
1 package (8 ounces) cream cheese, softened
1½ cups sugar
4 large eggs
1½ teaspoons vanilla extract
2 cups all-purpose flour
1½ teaspoons baking powder
½ teaspoon salt
2 cups fresh or frozen cranberries
½ cup chopped pecans
ICING
2 cups confectioners' sugar
3 tablespoons 2% milk

1. Preheat oven to 350°. In a large bowl, cream butter, cream cheese and sugar until light and fluffy. Add eggs, one at a time, beating well after each addition. Beat in vanilla. Combine flour, baking powder and salt; stir into the creamed mixture just until moistened. Fold in cranberries and pecans.

2. Fill greased or paper-lined muffin cups three-fourths full. Bake 20-25 minutes or until a toothpick inserted in the center of a muffin comes out clean. Cool in pans for 5 minutes before removing to wire racks.

3. Combine confectioners' sugar and milk; drizzle icing over the muffins.

NUTRITION FACTS 1 muffin: 105 cal., 6g fat (3g sat. fat), 46mg chol., 113mg sod., 10g carb. (1g sugars, 1g fiber), 3g pro.

TOP TIP

If your muffins form points, it's probably because you overmixed them. Generally, the dry ingredients should be combined first, then the liquids stirred in just until moistened. It's normal for a few lumps to remain in muffin batter.

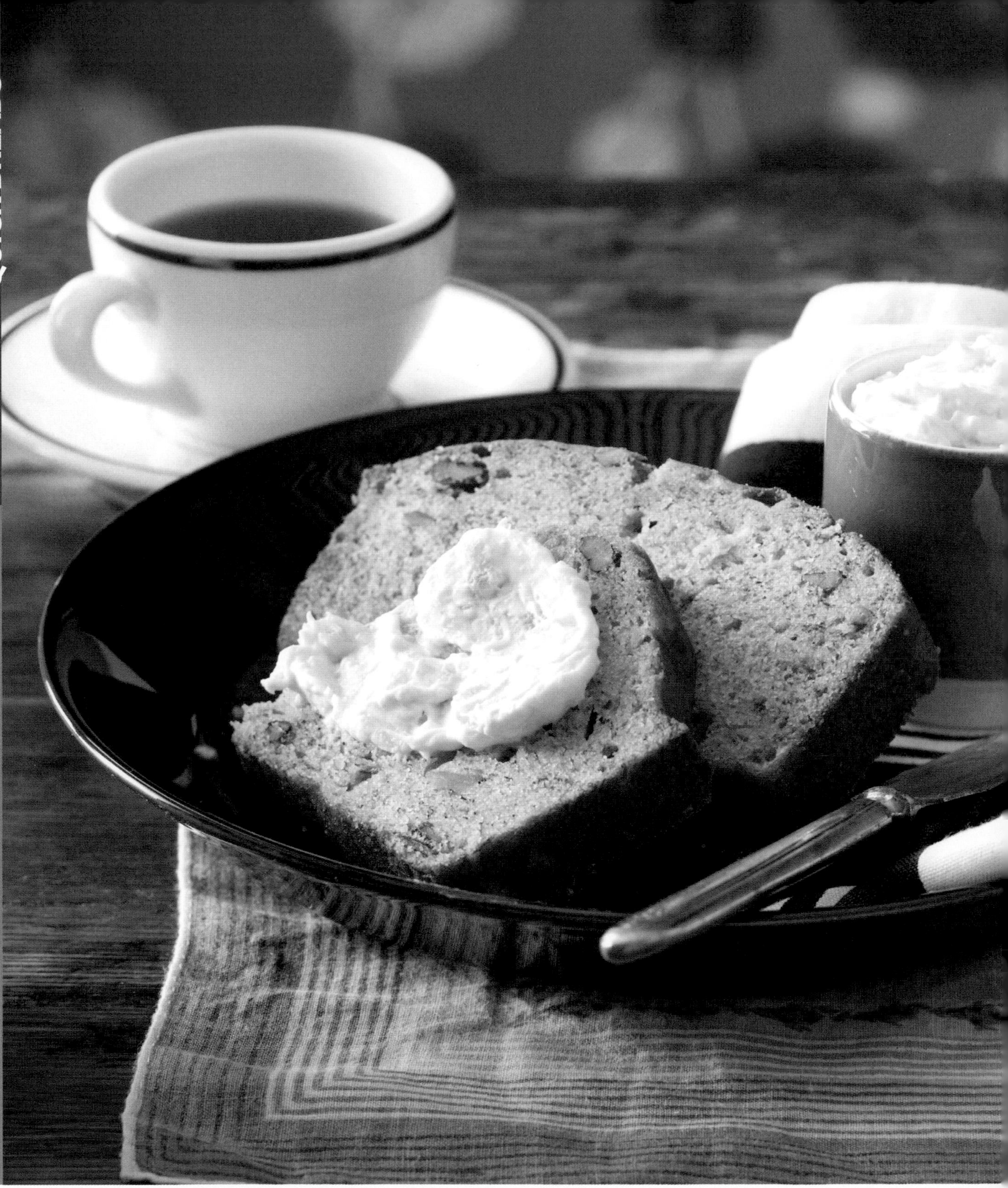

Banana Pecan Loaf

We slice this banana bread so thick it is almost embarrassing—but we need slices thick enough to deliver ample portions of the Pineapple Spread! When making the spread, beat the cream cheese until it's as light and fluffy as whipped cream.

—LEE ANN MILLER MILLERSBURG, OH

PREP: 25 MIN. • **BAKE:** 50 MIN + COOLING
MAKES: 1 LOAF (16 SLICES)

- ½ cup butter, softened
- 1 cup packed brown sugar
- 2 large eggs
- 3 medium ripe bananas, mashed
- 2 cups all-purpose flour
- ½ teaspoon baking powder
- ½ teaspoon baking soda
- ½ teaspoon salt
- ½ cup chopped pecans

PINEAPPLE SPREAD

- 1 package (8 ounces) cream cheese, softened
- 1 cup canned crushed pineapple, well drained

1. Preheat oven to 350°. In a large bowl, cream butter and sugar until light and fluffy. Add eggs, one at a time, beating well after each addition. Beat in bananas. Combine flour, baking powder, baking soda and salt; add to the creamed mixture. Fold in pecans.

2. Transfer to a greased 9x5-in. loaf pan. Bake for 50-60 minutes or until a toothpick inserted in the center comes out clean. Cool in the pan for 10 minutes before removing to a wire rack.

3. In a small bowl, combine cream cheese and pineapple. Serve with the bread.

NUTRITION FACTS 1 slice with 4½ teaspoons spread: 275 cal., 14g fat (7g sat. fat), 57mg chol., 223mg sod., 35g carb. (20g sugars, 1g fiber), 4g pro.

Garlic Herb Bubble Loaf, p. 71

CHAPTER 3

YEAST BREADS

Nothing beats the aroma of baking bread—except the taste!

Pumpkin Pan Rolls

Serve these spicy-sweet pumpkin rolls for dinner—or any time of day—and get ready to hear a chorus of yums in your kitchen!
—**LINNEA REIN** TOPEKA, KS

PREP: 20 MIN. + RISING • **BAKE:** 20 MIN.
MAKES: 20 ROLLS

¾ cup whole milk
⅓ cup packed brown sugar
5 tablespoons butter, divided
1 teaspoon salt
2 packages (¼ ounce each) active dry yeast
½ cup warm water (110° to 115°)
2 to 2½ cups all-purpose flour
1½ cups whole wheat flour
½ cup canned pumpkin
½ teaspoon ground cinnamon
¼ teaspoon ground ginger
¼ teaspoon ground nutmeg

1. In a small saucepan, heat milk, brown sugar, 4 tablespoons of butter and the salt to 110°-115°; set aside.

In a large bowl, dissolve yeast in warm water. Stir in the milk mixture. Add 1½ cups of all-purpose flour, whole wheat flour, pumpkin, cinnamon, ginger and nutmeg. Beat until smooth. Add enough of the remaining all-purpose flour to form a soft dough.

2. Turn dough onto a floured surface; knead until it is smooth and elastic, 6-8 minutes. Place in a greased bowl, turning once to grease top. Cover and let rise in a warm place until doubled, about 1 hour.

3. Punch dough down. Divide into 20 pieces; shape into balls. Place in a greased 13x9-in. baking pan. Cover and let rise for 30 minutes or until doubled.

4. Melt remaining butter; brush over dough. Bake at 375° for 20-25 minutes or until golden brown. Remove from pan to a wire rack. Serve warm.

NUTRITION FACTS 1 roll: 124 cal., 3g fat (2g sat. fat), 9mg chol., 154mg sod., 21g carb. (5g sugars, 2g fiber), 3g pro. *Diabetic Exchanges:* 1½ starch, ½ fat.

Khachapuri

In Russia, my husband and I discovered these marvelous cheese pies. The traditional pastries can also be made bite-sized.
—**RACHEL SAUDER** TREMONT, IL

PREP: 30 MIN. + RISING • **BAKE:** 30 MIN.
MAKES: 6 SERVINGS

3½ teaspoons active dry yeast
¾ cup warm whole milk
    (110° to 115°)
6 tablespoons butter, melted
2 tablespoons honey
2 to 2½ cups all-purpose flour
1 teaspoon salt
¼ teaspoon ground coriander
FILLING
1 large egg, lightly beaten
12 ounces brick cheese, shredded

1. In a large bowl, dissolve the yeast in warm milk. Stir in butter and honey. In another bowl, combine 1¾ cups of flour, salt and coriander; gradually add to the yeast mixture, beating until smooth. Stir in enough of the remaining flour to form a soft dough.

2. Turn dough onto a lightly floured surface; knead until smooth and elastic, 6-8 minutes. Place in a greased bowl, turning once to grease the top. Cover and let rise in a warm place until doubled, about 1 hour.

3. Punch dough down. Let rise until doubled, about 30 minutes. Turn onto a lightly floured surface; divide into six balls. Roll each ball into a 6½-in. circle.

4. In a small bowl, combine egg and cheese. Mound about ½ cup of the cheese mixture in the center of each circle. Fold the dough over the filling, gathering and twisting into a knot to seal. Place on an ungreased baking sheet. Let stand for 10 minutes. Bake at 375° for 30-35 minutes or until lightly browned. Serve immediately.

NUTRITION FACTS 1 roll: 511 cal., 30g fat (18g sat. fat), 128mg chol., 820mg sod., 42g carb. (8g sugars, 2g fiber), 21g pro.

DID YOU KNOW?

Yeast can be purchased three ways—in individual packages, in bulk or in cake form. Each ¼-ounce package of active dry yeast is equal to 2¼ teaspoons of bulk yeast or one fresh cake yeast (0.6 ounce).

Caraway Seed Rye Bread

It was probably 45 years ago when the threshers came to dinner and Mother served this bread. Every time I bake it, I get nostalgic for those days. My parents emigrated from Czechoslovakia and couldn't speak English very well. The threshers hardly talked anyway—they were too busy enjoying Mother's delicious food!
—**MILLIE FEATHER** BARODA, MI

PREP: 20 MIN. + RISING • **BAKE:** 25 MIN.
MAKES: 2 LOAVES (10 SLICES EACH)

   2   packages (¼ ounce each) active dry yeast
   2   cups warm water (110° to 115°), divided
   ¼   cup packed brown sugar
   1   tablespoon caraway seeds
   1   tablespoon canola oil
   2   teaspoons salt
   2½ cups rye flour
   2¾ to 3¼ cups all-purpose flour, divided

1. In a large bowl, dissolve yeast in ½ cup warm water. Add brown sugar, caraway, oil, salt and the remaining water; mix well. Stir in rye flour and 1 cup all-purpose flour; beat until smooth. Add enough of the remaining all-purpose flour to form a soft dough.

2. Turn dough onto a floured surface; knead until it is smooth and elastic, 6-8 minutes. Place in a greased bowl, turning once to grease top. Cover and let rise in a warm place until doubled, about 1 hour.

3. Punch dough down; divide in half. Shape each half into a ball; place in two greased 8-in. round baking pans or ovenproof skillets. Flatten balls to a 6-in. diameter. Cover and let rise until nearly doubled, about 30 minutes. Bake at 375° for 25-30 minutes or until golden brown.

NUTRITION FACTS 1 slice: 126 cal., 1g fat (0 sat. fat), 0 chol., 238mg sod., 26g carb. (4g sugars, 3g fiber), 3g pro.

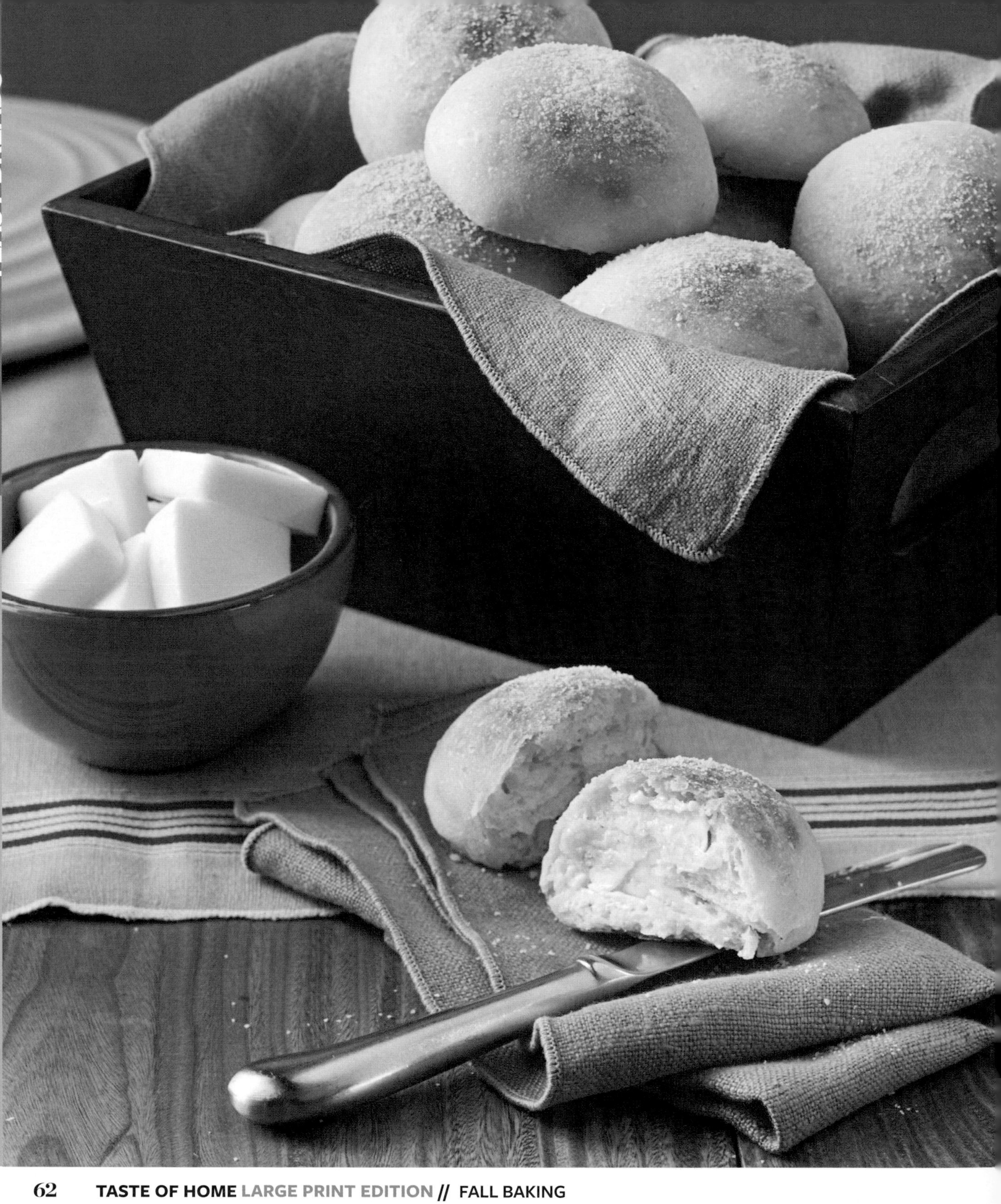

Cornmeal Dinner Rolls

An ideal sidekick to chili, soups and stews, these biscuits can also stand alone with a simple pat of butter and drizzle of honey.
—**BRYNN RADER** OLYMPIA, WA

PREP: 35 MIN.+ RISING • **BAKE:** 15 MIN.
MAKES: 2½ DOZEN

- 2 cups whole milk
- ½ cup sugar
- ½ cup butter, cubed
- ⅓ cup cornmeal
- 1¼ teaspoons salt
- 1 package (¼ ounce) active dry yeast
- ¼ cup warm water (110° to 115°)
- 2 large eggs
- 4¾ to 5¾ cups all-purpose flour

TOPPING
- 2 tablespoons butter, melted
- 1 tablespoon cornmeal

1. In a large saucepan, combine milk, sugar, butter, cornmeal and salt. Bring to a boil over medium heat, stirring constantly. Reduce heat; cook and stir 5-8 minutes or until thickened. Cool to 110°-115°.

2. In a small bowl, dissolve yeast in warm water. In a large bowl, combine the eggs, cornmeal mixture, yeast mixture and 2 cups of flour; beat until smooth. Stir in enough of the remaining flour to form a soft dough (dough will be sticky).

3. Turn dough onto a floured surface; knead until it is smooth and elastic, 6-8 minutes. Place in a greased bowl, turning once to grease the top. Cover with plastic wrap; let rise in a warm place until doubled, about 1 hour.

4. Punch dough down. Turn onto a lightly floured surface; divide into 30 balls. Place 2 in. apart on greased baking sheets. Cover with a clean kitchen towel; let rise in a warm place until doubled, about 45 minutes.

5. Uncover rolls; brush with melted butter and sprinkle with cornmeal. Bake at 375° for 13-17 minutes or until golden brown. Remove from pans to wire racks; serve warm.

NUTRITION FACTS 1 roll: 140 cal., 5g fat (3g sat. fat), 26mg chol., 137mg sod., 21g carb. (4g sugars, 1g fiber), 3g pro.

Soft Oatmeal Bread

My husband loves to make this bread. With its mild oat taste and soft texture, it's a hit with the whole family. Try toasting slices for a not-too-sweet breakfast treat.

—NANCY MONTGOMERY PLAINWELL, MI

PREP: 10 MIN. • **BAKE:** 3 HOURS
MAKES: 1 LOAF (20 SLICES)

1½ cups water (70° to 80°)
¼ cup canola oil
1 teaspoon lemon juice
¼ cup sugar
2 teaspoons salt
3 cups all-purpose flour
1½ cups quick-cooking oats
2½ teaspoons active dry yeast

1. In bread machine pan, place all ingredients in order suggested by the manufacturer. Select basic bread setting. Choose crust color and loaf size if available.

2. Bake according to bread machine directions (check dough after 5 minutes of mixing; add 1-2 tablespoons of water or flour if needed).

FREEZE OPTION Securely wrap and freeze cooled loaf in foil and place in resealable plastic freezer bag. To use, thaw at room temperature.

NUTRITION FACTS 1 slice: 127 cal., 3g fat (0 sat. fat), 0 chol., 237mg sod., 21g carb. (3g sugars, 1g fiber), 3g pro.

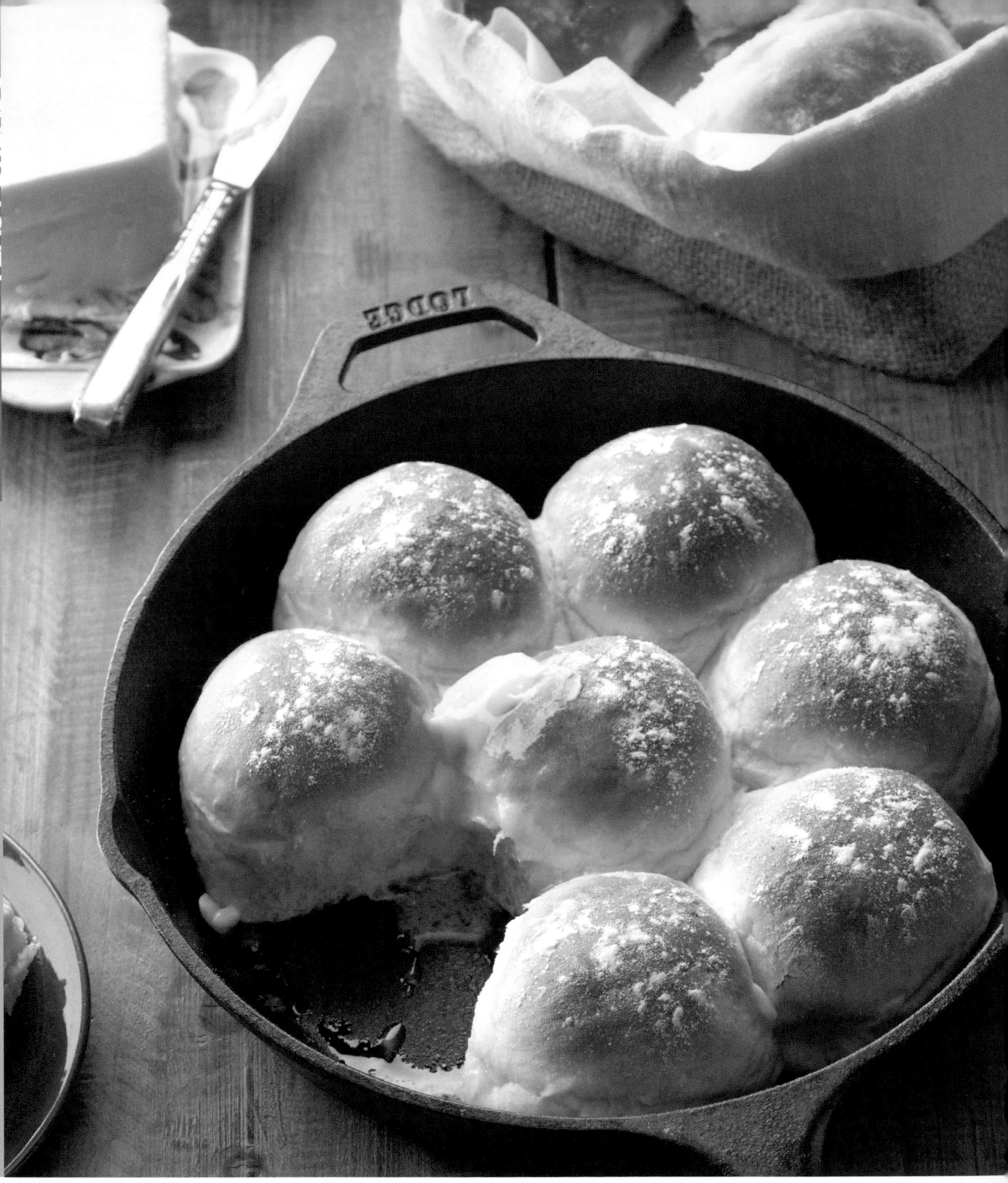

Potato Pan Rolls

My family loves these rolls and requests them often. I'm happy to oblige, because the rolls don't take long to make—they use quick-rise yeast.

—**CONNIE STORCKMAN** EVANSTON, WY

PREP: 15 MIN. + RISING • **BAKE:** 20 MIN.
MAKES: 16 ROLLS

4½ to 5 cups all-purpose flour
  3 tablespoons sugar
  2 packages (¼ ounce each)
    quick-rise yeast
1½ teaspoons salt
1¼ cups water
  3 tablespoons butter
 ½ cup mashed potatoes (without
    added milk and butter)
    Additional all-purpose flour

1. In a large bowl, combine 2 cups of flour, sugar, yeast and salt. In a small saucepan, heat water and butter to 120°-130°. Add to the dry ingredients; beat until smooth. Stir in mashed potatoes and enough of the remaining flour to form a soft dough.

2. Turn dough onto a floured surface; knead until it is smooth and elastic, 6-8 minutes. Cover and let rest for 10 minutes. Divide into 16 pieces. Shape each piece into a ball. Place in two greased 8- or 9-in. round baking pans or ovenproof skillets. Cover and let rise in a warm place until doubled, about 30 minutes.

3. Sprinkle tops of rolls with additional flour. Bake at 400° for 18-22 minutes or until golden brown. Remove from pans to wire racks.

NUTRITION FACTS 1 roll: 163 cal., 3g fat (1g sat. fat), 6mg chol., 239mg sod., 30g carb. (3g sugars, 1g fiber), 4g pro.

TOP TIP

You can use bread flour for all-purpose flour in yeast-raised doughs. Store bread flour in an airtight container in a cool, dry place for 10-15 months, or in the freezer for longer. Cold flour slows the dough's rising; warm it to room temperature before using.

Sweet Potato Crescents

These light-as-air crescent rolls make a delightful accompaniment to any menu. I often serve them as part of our Thanksgiving dinner.

—REBECCA BAILEY FAIRBURY, NE

PREP: 30 MIN. + RISING • **BAKE:** 15 MIN.
MAKES: 3 DOZEN

- 2 packages (¼ ounce each) active dry yeast
- 1 cup warm water (110° to 115°)
- 1 can (15¾ ounces) cut sweet potatoes, drained and mashed
- ½ cup sugar
- ½ cup shortening
- 1 large egg
- 1½ teaspoons salt
- 5 to 5½ cups all-purpose flour
- ¼ cup butter, melted

1. In a large bowl, dissolve yeast in water; let stand for 5 minutes. Beat in sweet potatoes, sugar, shortening, egg, salt and 3 cups of flour. Add enough of the remaining flour to form a stiff dough.

2. Turn dough onto a floured surface; knead until it is smooth and elastic, 6-8 minutes. Place in a greased bowl, turning once to grease top. Cover and let rise in a warm place until doubled, about 1 hour.

3. Punch dough down; divide into thirds. Roll each portion into a 12-in. circle; cut each into 12 wedges. Brush with butter. Roll up from the wide end and place, pointed end down, 2 in. apart on greased baking sheets. Cover and let rise until doubled, about 40 minutes.

4. Bake at 375° for 13-15 minutes or until golden brown. Remove from pans to wire racks.

NUTRITION FACTS 1 crescent: 123 cal., 4g fat (2g sat. fat), 9mg chol., 119mg sod., 19g carb. (5g sugars, 1g fiber), 2g pro.

Garlic Herb Bubble Loaf

I adapted an old sour cream bread recipe for this deliciously different pull-apart loaf that smells heavenly while baking. It has a light crust, tender interior and lots of herb and butter flavor. It's wonderful with a hot bowl of potato soup.

—**KATIE CRILL** PRIEST RIVER, ID

PREP: 25 MIN. + RISING • **BAKE:** 35 MIN.
MAKES: 1 LOAF (36 PIECES)

½ cup water (70° to 80°)
½ cup sour cream
2 tablespoons butter, softened
3 tablespoons sugar
1½ teaspoons salt
3 cups bread flour
2¼ teaspoons active dry yeast

GARLIC HERB BUTTER
¼ cup butter, melted
4 garlic cloves, minced
¼ teaspoon each dried oregano,
  thyme and rosemary, crushed

1. In bread machine pan, place the first seven ingredients in order suggested by the manufacturer. Select dough setting. Check dough after 5 minutes of mixing; add 1-2 tablespoons of water or flour if needed.

2. When cycle is completed, turn dough onto a lightly floured surface. Cover and let rest for 15 minutes. Divide dough into 36 pieces. Shape each piece into a ball. In a shallow bowl, combine butter, garlic and herbs. Dip each ball in the butter mixture; place in an ungreased 9x5-in. loaf pan. Cover and let rise in a warm place until doubled, about 45 minutes.

3. Bake at 375° for 35-40 minutes or until golden brown (cover loosely with foil if bread browns too quickly). Remove from pan to a wire rack. Serve warm.

NOTE We recommend you do not use a bread machine's time-delay feature for this recipe.

NUTRITION FACTS 1 piece: 141 cal., 6g fat (3g sat. fat), 12mg chol., 230mg sod., 19g carb. (2g sugars, 1g fiber), 3g pro.

Honey Wheat Loaves

This recipe makes four loaves, so you can serve one with dinner and give the others as gifts! This bread is tender and chewy with a hint of sweetness.

—**ROGER HAWLEY** VALLEY PARK, MO

PREP: 45 MIN. + RISING
BAKE: 30 MIN. + COOLING
MAKES: 4 LOAVES (16 SLICES EACH)

3	packages (¼ ounce each) active dry yeast
5	cups warm water (110° to 115°), divided
1	tablespoon plus ⅔ cup honey, divided
⅔	cup canola oil
½	cup sugar
2	teaspoons salt
4	cups whole wheat flour
1	cup toasted wheat germ
6	to 8 cups bread flour

1. In a large bowl, dissolve yeast in ¾ cup warm water and 1 tablespoon honey. Add the remaining water and honey, the oil, sugar, salt, whole wheat flour, wheat germ and 3 cups of bread flour. Beat until smooth. Stir in enough of the remaining bread flour to form a soft dough (dough will be sticky).

2. Turn dough onto a lightly floured surface; knead until smooth and elastic, 6-8 minutes. Place in a bowl coated with cooking spray, turning once to coat the top. Cover and let rise in a warm place until doubled, about 1 hour.

3. Punch dough down. Shape into four loaves. Place in 9x5-in. loaf pans coated with cooking spray. Cover and let rise until nearly doubled, about 30 minutes.

4. Bake at 350° for 30-35 minutes or until golden brown. Remove from pans to wire racks to cool.

NUTRITION FACTS 1 slice: 108 cal., 3g fat (0 sat. fat), 0 chol., 75mg sod., 19g carb. (5g sugars, 1g fiber), 3g pro. *Diabetic Exchanges:* 1½ starch, ½ fat.

HOW TO

RISE DOUGH IN THE OVEN

Try these two methods: 1. Cover the bowl of dough with a clean kitchen towel and set it on the top rack in a cold oven. Place a pan of steaming hot water underneath the bowl; close the oven door. 2. Turn your oven to its lowest setting for 50 seconds, then turn off the heat. Place the covered bowl of dough in the oven; close the oven door.

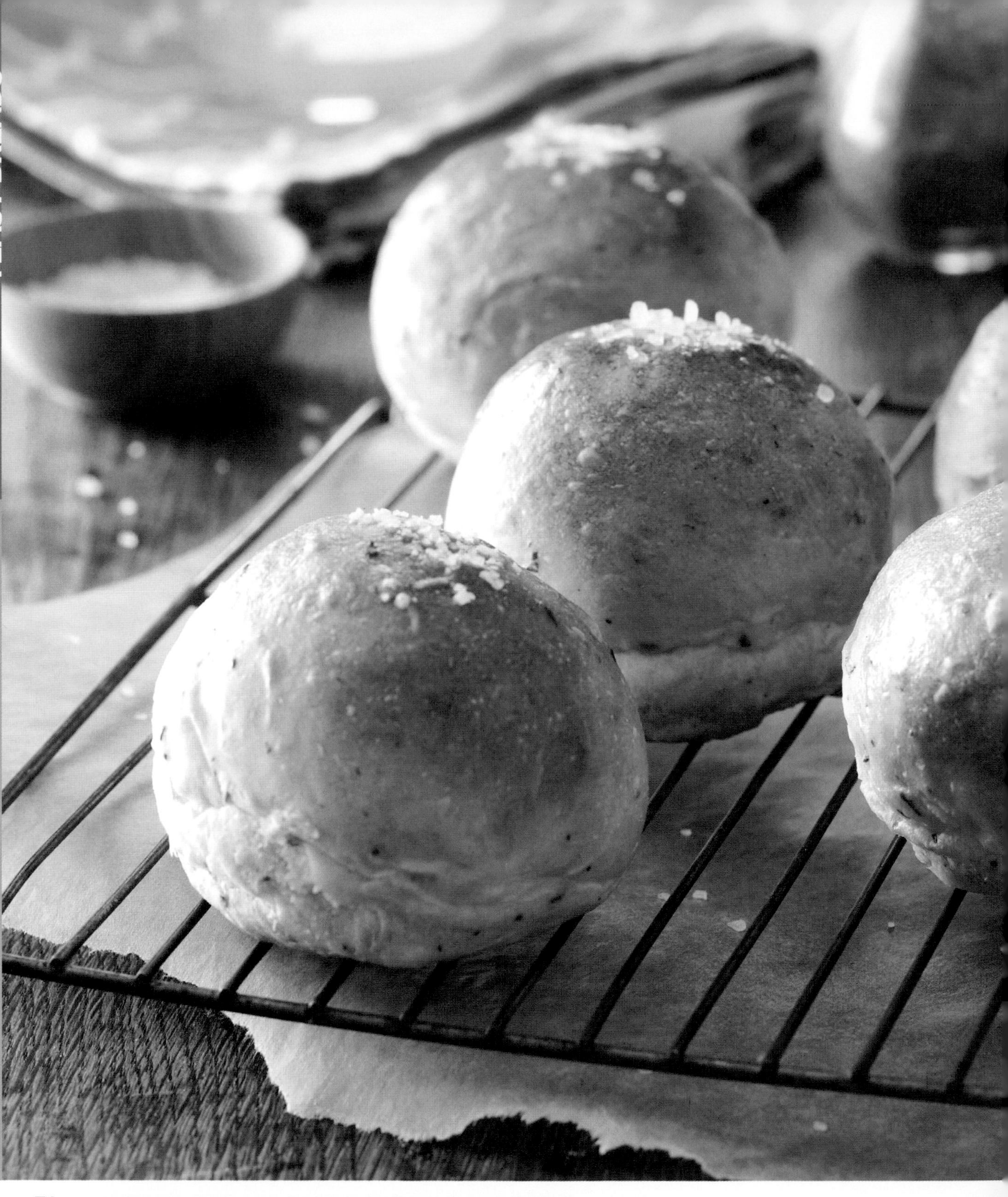

Herbed Dinner Rolls

After I had my sixth child, a friend dropped off dinner, including these rolls, which start in a bread machine. They were so yeasty-good that I soon bought my own machine so I could make them myself.

—DANA LOWRY HICKORY, NC

PREP: 20 MIN. + RISING • **BAKE:** 15 MIN.
MAKES: 16 ROLLS

1	cup water (70° to 80°)
2	tablespoons butter, softened
1	large egg
¼	cup sugar
1	teaspoon salt
½	teaspoon each dried basil, oregano, thyme and rosemary, crushed
3¼	cups bread flour
2¼	teaspoons active dry yeast
	Additional butter, melted
	Coarse salt, optional

1. In a bread machine pan, place water, butter, egg, sugar, salt, seasonings, flour and yeast in order suggested by the manufacturer. Select dough setting. Check dough after 5 minutes of mixing; add 1 to 2 tablespoons of water or flour if needed.

2. When cycle is complete, turn dough onto a lightly floured surface. Divide dough into 16 portions; shape each into a ball. Place 2 in. apart on greased baking sheets. Cover and let rise in a warm place until doubled, about 30 minutes.

3. Bake at 375° for 12-15 minutes or until golden brown. Brush with butter and sprinkle with coarse salt if desired. Remove from pans to wire racks.

NOTE We recommend you do not use a bread machine's time-delay feature for this recipe.

NUTRITION FACTS 1 roll: 112 cal., 2g fat (1g sat. fat), 17mg chol., 166mg sod., 21g carb. (3g sugars, 1g fiber), 4g pro.

Peppy Cheese Bread

As the stay-at-home mother of two little girls, I pack a lot of activity into my days. The bread machine makes it a snap for me to turn out this attractive loaf that gets its zip from cayenne pepper, pepperoni and Mexican cheese.

—DUSTI CHRISTENSEN GOODRIDGE, MN

PREP: 10 MIN. • **BAKE:** 4 HOURS
MAKES: 1 LOAF (16 SLICES)

- 1   cup water (70° to 80°)
- 1   tablespoon butter
- 2   tablespoons sugar
- 2   teaspoons ground mustard
- ½   teaspoon salt
- ½   teaspoon cayenne pepper
- ¼   teaspoon garlic powder
- 3   cups bread flour
- 2¼ teaspoons active dry yeast
- 1½ cups shredded Mexican cheese blend
- 1   cup chopped pepperoni

1. In bread machine pan, place the first nine ingredients in the order suggested by the manufacturer. Select basic bread setting. Choose crust color and loaf size if available. Bake according to bread machine directions. Check dough after 5 minutes of mixing; add 1-2 tablespoons of water or flour if needed.

2. Just before the final kneading (your machine may audibly signal this), add the cheese and pepperoni.

FREEZE OPTION Securely wrap cooled loaf in foil and place in resealable plastic freezer bag to freeze. To use, thaw at room temperature.

NOTE We recommend you do not use a bread machine's time-delay feature for this recipe.

NUTRITION FACTS 1 slice: 177 cal., 8g fat (4g sat. fat), 19mg chol., 329mg sod., 19g carb. (2g sugars, 1g fiber), 7g pro.

Walnut-Filled Pillows, p. 99

CHAPTER 4

COOKIES

Small and sweet; fun or elegant...cookies are the perfect indulgence.

Cranberry Lemon Sandwiches

I bake cookies all year long, so my friends and family call me the cookie lady! When I bake these for Christmas, I make three batches—one for my husband and two to give as gifts.

—PATRICIA MICHALSKI OSWEGO, NY

PREP: 20 MIN. + CHILLING
BAKE: 15 MIN./BATCH
MAKES: ABOUT 4½ DOZEN

1 cup butter, softened
1 cup shortening
1 cup sugar
1 cup confectioners' sugar
2 large eggs
2 teaspoons vanilla extract
4 cups all-purpose flour
1 teaspoon cream of tartar
1 teaspoon grated lemon peel
½ teaspoon salt
¾ cup dried cranberries

FILLING
⅔ cup butter, softened
2¾ cups confectioners' sugar
¼ cup 2% milk
1¼ teaspoons grated lemon peel

1. In a large bowl, cream butter, shortening and sugars until light and fluffy. Add eggs, one at a time, beating well after each addition. Beat in vanilla. Combine flour, cream of tartar, lemon peel and salt; gradually add to the creamed mixture and mix well. Stir in cranberries. Cover and refrigerate for 2 hours or until easy to handle.

2. Preheat oven to 350°. Roll dough into 1-in. balls. Place 2 in. apart on ungreased baking sheets. Flatten with a glass dipped in sugar. Bake for 12-14 minutes or until edges are lightly browned. Remove to wire racks to cool.

3. In a small bowl, combine the filling ingredients; beat until smooth. Spread on the bottoms of half of the cookies; top with the remaining cookies.

NUTRITION FACTS 2 sandwich cookies: 343 cal., 19g fat (9g sat. fat), 46mg chol., 164mg sod., 41g carb. (25g sugars, 1g fiber), 3g pro.

Giant Molasses Cookies

My family always requests these soft and deliciously chewy treats. The cookies are also great for shipping as holiday gifts or to troops overseas.

—KRISTINE CHAYES SMITHTOWN, NY

PREP: 30 MIN. • **BAKE:** 15 MIN./BATCH
MAKES: 2 DOZEN

1½ cups butter, softened
 2 cups sugar
 2 large eggs
 ½ cup molasses
4½ cups all-purpose flour
 4 teaspoons ground ginger
 2 teaspoons baking soda
1½ teaspoons ground cinnamon
 1 teaspoon ground cloves
 ¼ teaspoon salt
 ¼ cup chopped pecans
 ¾ cup coarse sugar

1. Preheat oven to 350°. In a large bowl, cream butter and sugar until light and fluffy. Beat in eggs and molasses. Combine flour, ginger, baking soda, cinnamon, cloves and salt; gradually add to the creamed mixture and mix well. Fold in pecans.

2. Shape dough into 2-in. balls and roll in coarse sugar. Place 2½ in. apart on ungreased baking sheets. Bake for 13-15 minutes or until tops are cracked. Remove to wire racks to cool.

NUTRITION FACTS 1 cookie: 310 cal., 13g fat (7g sat. fat), 48mg chol., 219mg sod., 46g carb. (27g sugars, 1g fiber), 3g pro.

TOP TIP

When measuring molasses or other sticky ingredients, wipe the inside of your measuring cup with a paper towel coated in a little bit of vegetable oil. The oil releases the molasses from the cup so that you get every drop out, and it makes cleanup easier.

Chewy Good Oatmeal Cookies

Here's a great oatmeal cookie with all of my favorite extras: dried cherries, white chocolate chips and macadamia nuts.

—SANDY HARZ SPRING LAKE, MI

PREP: 20 MIN. • **BAKE:** 10 MIN./BATCH
MAKES: 3½ DOZEN

- 1 cup butter, softened
- 1 cup packed brown sugar
- ½ cup sugar
- 2 large eggs
- 1 tablespoon honey
- 2 teaspoons vanilla extract
- 2½ cups quick-cooking oats
- 1½ cups all-purpose flour
- 1 teaspoon baking soda
- ½ teaspoon salt
- ½ teaspoon ground cinnamon
- 1⅓ cups dried cherries
- 1 cup white baking chips
- 1 cup chopped macadamia nuts

1. Preheat oven to 350°. In a large bowl, cream butter and sugars until light and fluffy. Beat in eggs, honey and vanilla. In another bowl, mix oats, flour, baking soda, salt and cinnamon; gradually beat into the creamed mixture. Stir in the remaining ingredients.

2. Drop dough by rounded tablespoonfuls 2 in. apart onto greased baking sheets. Bake 10-12 minutes or until golden brown. Cool on pan 2 minutes; remove to wire racks to cool.

CHEWY CRANBERRY OATMEAL COOKIES Substitute dried cranberries for the dried cherries.

CHEWY OATMEAL CHIP COOKIES Omit the cinnamon, dried cherries and macadamia nuts. Add 1 cup each semisweet chocolate chips and butterscotch chips with the white baking chips.

NUTRITION FACTS 1 cookie: 161 cal., 8g fat (4g sat. fat), 22mg chol., 105mg sod., 20g carb. (13g sugars, 1g fiber), 2g pro.

Coffee Shortbread

When you need a treat for brunch, bake some of these tasty coffee-flavored cookies. The two-tone chocolate drizzle is surprisingly easy to do.

—**DIXIE TERRY** GOREVILLE, IL

PREP: 15 MIN.
BAKE: 20 MIN./BATCH + COOLING
MAKES: ABOUT 2½ DOZEN

1	cup butter, softened
½	cup packed brown sugar
¼	cup sugar
2	tablespoons instant coffee granules
¼	teaspoon salt
2	cups all-purpose flour
½	cup semisweet chocolate chips
2	teaspoons shortening, divided
½	cup white baking chips

1. Preheat oven to 300°. In a large bowl, cream butter, sugars, coffee granules and salt until light and fluffy; gradually beat flour into creamed mixture.

2. On a lightly floured surface, roll the dough to ¼-in. thickness. Cut with floured 2-in. cookie cutters. Place 2 in. apart on ungreased baking sheets.

3. Bake for 20-22 minutes or until set. Remove to wire racks to cool completely. In a microwave, melt chocolate chips and 1 teaspoon shortening; stir until smooth. Repeat with baking chips and remaining shortening. Drizzle each chocolate mixture over the cookies; refrigerate until set. Store cookies between pieces of waxed paper in an airtight container.

NUTRITION FACTS 1 cookie: 137 cal., 8g fat (5g sat. fat), 17mg chol., 73mg sod., 15g carb. (8g sugars, 0 fiber), 1g pro.

Chocolate Pistachio Biscotti

Chocolate, pistachios and cranberries are great together; adding the cranberries to this recipe made it not just sweeter but healthier, too. Biscotti, a traditional Italian cookie, is often served with coffee or sweet dessert wine—feel free to dip!

—**GILDA LESTER** MILLSBORO, DE

PREP: 30 MIN. • **BAKE:** 30 MIN. + COOLING
MAKES: 40 COOKIES

⅓ cup butter, softened
1 cup plus 1 tablespoon sugar, divided
3 large eggs
2 teaspoons vanilla extract
2¾ cups all-purpose flour
⅓ cup baking cocoa
2½ teaspoons baking powder
½ teaspoon ground cinnamon
1 cup semisweet chocolate chips
½ cup pistachios
½ cup dried cranberries

1. Preheat oven to 350°. In a large bowl, cream butter and 1 cup of sugar until light and fluffy. Add eggs, one at a time, beating well after each addition. Beat in vanilla. Mix flour, cocoa, baking powder and cinnamon; add to the creamed mixture and mix well (dough will be sticky). Stir in chocolate chips, pistachios and cranberries.

2. Divide the dough into four portions. On ungreased baking sheets, shape portions into 10x2½-in. rectangles. Sprinkle with the remaining sugar. Bake for 20-25 minutes or until set. Carefully remove to wire racks; cool for 5 minutes.

3. Transfer rectangles to a cutting board; cut each into 10 slices. Place slices cut side down on ungreased baking sheets. Bake 5-8 minutes on each side or until lightly browned. Remove to wire racks to cool. Store in an airtight container.

NUTRITION FACTS 1 biscotti: 107 cal., 4g fat (2g sat. fat), 20mg chol., 48mg sod., 17g carb. (9g sugars, 1g fiber), 2g pro. *Diabetic Exchanges:* 1 starch, 1 fat.

Lara's Tender Gingersnaps

Soft gingersnaps embody the tastes and smells of the Christmas season, but they really are perfect for any fall or winter gathering. I enjoy the blend of cloves, ginger and cinnamon in this delicious cookie.

—LARA PENNELL MAULDIN, SC

PREP: 15 MIN. + CHILLING
BAKE: 10 MIN./BATCH
MAKES: 3 DOZEN

- 1 cup packed brown sugar
- ¾ cup butter, melted
- 1 large egg
- ¼ cup molasses
- 2¼ cups all-purpose flour
- 1½ teaspoons ground ginger
- 1 teaspoon baking soda
- 1 teaspoon ground cinnamon
- ½ teaspoon ground cloves
- ¼ cup sugar

1. In a large bowl, beat brown sugar and butter until blended. Beat in egg and molasses. Combine flour, ginger, baking soda, cinnamon and cloves; gradually add to the brown sugar mixture and mix well (dough will be stiff). Cover and refrigerate for at least 2 hours.

2. Preheat oven to 350°. Shape dough into 1 in. balls. Roll in sugar. Place 2 in. apart on greased baking sheets.

3. Bake for 9-11 minutes or until set. Cool for 1 minute before removing from pans to wire racks.

NUTRITION FACTS 1 cookie: 99 cal., 4g fat (2g sat. fat), 16mg chol., 67mg sod., 15g carb. (9g sugars, 0 fiber), 1g pro. *Diabetic Exchanges:* 1 starch, ½ fat.

HOW TO

SOFTEN BROWN SUGAR

If your brown sugar has hardened, soften it in one of two ways: 1. Place a bread slice or an apple wedge in a covered container with the sugar for a few days. 2. Microwave on high for 20-30 seconds. Repeat if necessary, but watch carefully because the sugar will begin to melt. Always store brown sugar in an airtight container.

Fancy Peanut Butter Cookies

I always receive compliments on my moist and chewy peanut butter cookies. But when I want to make them even more special, I decorate them with a tasty frosting.
—**JANET HOOPER** FLORISSANT, CO

PREP: 30 MIN.
BAKE: 10 MIN./BATCH + COOLING
MAKES: 7½ DOZEN

- 1 cup shortening
- 1 cup peanut butter
- 1 cup sugar
- 1 cup packed brown sugar
- 2 large eggs
- ¼ cup 2% milk
- 2 teaspoons vanilla extract
- 3½ cups all-purpose flour
- 2 teaspoons baking soda
- 1 teaspoon salt

FROSTING
- ¼ cup butter, softened
- ¼ cup shortening
- ¼ cup peanut butter
- 4 cups confectioners' sugar
- ¼ cup 2% milk
- 1 teaspoon vanilla extract
   Dash salt

ICING
- ½ cup semisweet chocolate chips, melted
- 2 tablespoons 2% milk

1. Preheat oven to 375°. In a large bowl, cream shortening, peanut butter and the sugars until light and fluffy, about 4 minutes. Add eggs, one at a time, beating well after each addition. Beat in milk and vanilla. Combine flour, baking soda and salt; gradually add to the creamed mixture and mix well.

2. Roll dough into 1-in. balls. Place 2 in. apart on ungreased baking sheets. Bake for 10-12 minutes or until golden brown. Remove to wire racks.

3. For frosting, in a large bowl, cream butter, shortening, peanut butter and confectioners' sugar until light and fluffy. Beat in milk, vanilla and salt until smooth. Frost the cookies. For icing, combine melted chips and milk; drizzle over the frosting.

NOTE We do not recommend reduced-fat peanut butter for this recipe.

NUTRITION FACTS 2 cookies: 227 cal., 11g fat (3g sat. fat), 13mg chol., 162mg sod., 30g carb. (21g sugars, 1g fiber), 3g pro.

Big & Buttery Chocolate Chip Cookies

Our version of the classic cookie is based on a recipe from the Hungry Bear bakery in California. These big, thick and chewy cookies are perfect for dunking!

—IRENE YEH MEQUON, WI

PREP: 35 MIN. + CHILLING
BAKE: 10 MIN./BATCH
MAKES: ABOUT 2 DOZEN

- 1 cup butter, softened
- 1 cup packed brown sugar
- ¾ cup sugar
- 2 large eggs
- 1½ teaspoons vanilla extract
- 2⅔ cups all-purpose flour
- 1¼ teaspoons baking soda
- 1 teaspoon salt
- 1 package (12 ounces) semisweet chocolate chips
- 2 cups coarsely chopped walnuts, toasted

1. In a large bowl, beat butter and sugars until blended. Beat in eggs and vanilla. In a small bowl, whisk flour, baking soda and salt; gradually beat into the butter mixture. Stir in chocolate chips and chopped walnuts.

2. Shape ¼ cupfuls of dough into balls. Flatten each ball to ¾-in. thickness (2½-in. diameter), smoothing edges as necessary. Place in an airtight container, separating the layers with waxed or parchment paper; refrigerate, covered, overnight.

3. To bake, place dough portions 2 in. apart on parchment paper-lined baking sheets; let stand at room temperature for 30 minutes before baking. Preheat oven to 400°.

4. Bake for 10-12 minutes or until the edges are golden brown (centers will be light). Cool on pans 2 minutes. Remove to wire racks to cool.

ALMOND CHOCOLATE CHIP COOKIES
Reduce vanilla to 1 teaspoon and add ¼ teaspoon almond extract. Substitute toasted almonds for the walnuts.

CHERRY CHOCOLATE CHIP COOKIES
Substitute 1 cup chopped dried cherries for 1 cup of the walnuts.

NOTE To toast nuts, bake in a shallow pan in a 350° oven for 5-10 minutes or cook in a skillet over low heat until lightly browned, stirring occasionally.

NUTRITION FACTS 1 cookie: 311 cal., 19g fat (8g sat. fat), 38mg chol., 229mg sod., 35g carb. (23g sugars, 2g fiber), 4g pro.

COOKIES

Mini Peanut Butter Sandwich Cookies

Peanut butter lovers go nuts for these rich little sandwich cookies. They're perfect for fall, but you can make them into a cool summer treat by sandwiching ice cream instead of frosting between the cookies.

—KERI WOLFE NAPPANEE, IN

PREP: 25 MIN.
BAKE: 15 MIN./BATCH + COOLING
MAKES: ABOUT 3½ DOZEN

1 cup shortening
1 cup creamy peanut butter
1 cup sugar
1 cup packed brown sugar
3 large eggs
1 teaspoon vanilla extract
3½ cups all-purpose flour
2 teaspoons baking soda
½ teaspoon salt

FILLING
¾ cup creamy peanut butter
½ cup 2% milk
1½ teaspoons vanilla extract
4 cups confectioners' sugar

1. Preheat oven to 350°. In a large bowl, cream shortening, peanut butter and sugars until blended. Beat in eggs and vanilla. In another bowl, whisk flour, baking soda and salt; gradually beat into creamed mixture.

2. Shape into 1-in. balls; place 2 in. apart on ungreased baking sheets. Bake for 11-13 minutes or until set. Remove from pans to wire racks to cool completely.

3. In a small bowl, beat peanut butter, milk and vanilla until blended. Beat in confectioners' sugar until smooth. Spread filling on bottoms of half of the cookies; cover with remaining cookies.

FREEZE OPTION Freeze unfilled cookies in freezer containers. To use, thaw the cookies and fill as directed.

NOTE Reduced-fat peanut butter is not recommended for this recipe.

NUTRITION FACTS 1 sandwich cookie: 240 cal., 11g fat (2g sat. fat), 14mg chol., 145mg sod., 33g carb. (23g sugars, 1g fiber), 4g pro.

Walnut-Filled Pillows

These tender cookie pillows filled with a delicious walnut mixture are my husband's favorite. He says it wouldn't be Christmas without them—but they're good any other time of year, too!

—NANCY KOSTREJ CANONSBURG, PA

PREP: 30 MIN. + CHILLING
BAKE: 10 MIN./BATCH
MAKES: 28 COOKIES

½ cup cold butter, cubed
1 package (3 ounces) cold cream cheese
1¼ cups all-purpose flour
¾ cup ground walnuts
¼ cup sugar
2 tablespoons whole milk
½ teaspoon vanilla or almond extract
1 large egg, lightly beaten
   Confectioners' sugar

1. In a large bowl, cut butter and cream cheese into flour until mixture resembles coarse crumbs. Blend the mixture until smooth dough forms, about 3 minutes. Pat into a rectangle; wrap in plastic wrap. Refrigerate for 1 hour or until firm. For filling, combine walnuts, sugar, milk and vanilla.

2. Preheat oven to 375°. Unwrap dough and place it on a lightly floured surface. Roll into a 17½x10-in. rectangle; cut into 2½-in. squares. Place a level teaspoonful of filling in the center of each square. Moisten the edges with water; fold in half and seal with a fork. Place 1 in. apart on ungreased baking sheets. Brush with egg.

3. Bake for 10-12 minutes or until edges are golden brown. Remove to wire racks to cool. Dust with confectioners' sugar.

NUTRITION FACTS 1 cookie: 84 cal., 6g fat (3g sat. fat), 20mg chol., 45mg sod., 6g carb. (2g sugars, 0 fiber), 1g pro.

Chocolate-Peanut Butter Cup Cookies

If you plan to enjoy one of these soft, fully loaded treats the day after you make them, you'd better find a good hiding spot.
—**JENNIFER KREY** CLARENCE, NY

PREP: 25 MIN. • **BAKE:** 10 MIN./BATCH
MAKES: 4 DOZEN

1 cup butter, softened
¾ cup creamy peanut butter
1 cup packed brown sugar
½ cup sugar
2 large egg yolks
¼ cup 2% milk
2 teaspoons vanilla extract
2⅓ cups all-purpose flour
⅓ cup baking cocoa
1 teaspoon baking soda
1 cup milk chocolate chips
1 cup peanut butter chips
6 packages (1½ ounces each) peanut butter cups, chopped

1. Preheat oven to 350°. In a large bowl, cream butter, peanut butter and sugars until light and fluffy. Beat in egg yolks, milk and vanilla. Combine flour, cocoa and baking soda; gradually add to creamed mixture and mix well. Stir in chips and peanut butter cups.

2. Drop heaping tablespoonfuls 2 in. apart onto ungreased baking sheets. Bake 8-10 minutes or until set (do not overbake). Cool 2 minutes before removing from pans to wire racks. Store in an airtight container.

NUTRITION FACTS 1 cookie: 170 cal., 10g fat (4g sat. fat), 20mg chol., 100mg sod., 18g carb. (12g sugars, 1g fiber), 3g pro.

DID YOU KNOW?

While baking soda is a single-ingredient item—sodium bicarbonate—baking powder combines baking soda and two other acids to extend the time of the leavening process. Simply put, baking powder allows cookies to rise; baking soda allows them to spread.

Cranberry Cookies with Browned Butter Glaze

I won a baking contest with these glazed soft cookies, which are so easy to make that just about anyone can pull them off. The fresh cranberries make them perfect for the holidays.

—LAURIE CORNETT CHARLEVOIX, MI

PREP: 40 MIN.
BAKE: 10 MIN./BATCH + COOLING
MAKES: ABOUT 4½ DOZEN

½ cup butter, softened
1 cup sugar
¾ cup packed brown sugar
1 large egg
2 tablespoons orange juice
3 cups all-purpose flour
1 teaspoon baking powder
½ teaspoon salt
¼ teaspoon baking soda
¼ cup 2% milk
2½ cups coarsely chopped fresh
     cranberries
1 cup white baking chips
1 cup chopped pecans or walnuts
GLAZE
⅓ cup butter, cubed
2 cups confectioners' sugar
1½ teaspoons vanilla extract
3 to 4 tablespoons water

1. Preheat oven to 375°. In a large bowl, cream butter and sugars until light and fluffy. Beat in egg and orange juice. In another bowl, whisk flour, baking powder, salt and baking soda; add to creamed mixture alternately with milk. Stir in cranberries, baking chips and pecans.

2. Drop dough by level tablespoonfuls 1 in. apart onto greased baking sheets. Bake 10-12 minutes or until light brown. Remove cookies from pans to wire racks to cool completely.

3. For glaze, in a small heavy saucepan, melt butter over medium heat. Heat for 5-7 minutes or until golden brown, stirring constantly. Remove from heat. Stir in confectioners' sugar, vanilla and enough water to reach a drizzling consistency. Drizzle over the cookies. Let stand until set.

NUTRITION FACTS 1 cookie: 130 cal., 5g fat (3g sat. fat), 12mg chol., 66mg sod., 19g carb. (13g sugars, 1g fiber), 1g pro.

**Pumpkin Pie
Squares, p. 114**

CHAPTER 5

BROWNIES & BARS

A cross between cookies and cakes, no-fuss bars make sweet sensations.

Cappuccino Cake Brownies

The perfect sweet for coffee lovers, these no-nut brownies combine a mild coffee flavor with the richness of chocolate. They're a quick and easy anytime snack or dessert.

—MARY HOUCHIN LEBANON, IL

PREP: 15 MIN. • **BAKE:** 25 MIN. + COOLING
MAKES: 16 BROWNIES

- 1   tablespoon instant coffee granules
- 2   teaspoons boiling water
- 1   cup semisweet chocolate chips
- ¼   cup butter, softened
- ½   cup sugar
- 2   large eggs
- ½   cup all-purpose flour
- ¼   teaspoon ground cinnamon

1. Preheat oven to 350°. In a small bowl, dissolve coffee in water; set aside. In a microwave, melt chocolate chips; stir until smooth. In a small bowl, cream butter and sugar until light and fluffy. Beat in eggs, melted chocolate and coffee mixture. Combine flour and cinnamon; gradually add to the creamed mixture until blended.

2. Pour into a greased 8-in. square baking pan. Bake for 25-30 minutes or until a toothpick inserted in the center comes out clean. Cool on a wire rack. Cut into squares.

NUTRITION FACTS 1 brownie: 124 cal., 7g fat (4g sat. fat), 34mg chol., 38mg sod., 16g carb. (12g sugars, 1g fiber), 2g pro.

TOP TIP

When melting chocolate chips, be sure the bowl and utensils are dry; any moisture may cause the chocolate to stiffen or "seize." Chocolate that has seized can sometimes be saved by immediately adding 1 tablespoon vegetable oil for each 6 ounces of chocolate. Slowly heat the mixture and stir until smooth.

Black-Bottom Banana Bars

These bars stay moist, and their banana-chocolate taste is even better the second day. My mother-in-law gave me this recipe, and it's a big favorite with my husband and our two sons.

—RENEE WRIGHT FERRYVILLE, WI

PREP: 20 MIN. • **BAKE:** 25 MIN.
MAKES: 3 DOZEN

½ cup butter, softened
1 cup sugar
1 large egg
1 teaspoon vanilla extract
1½ cups mashed ripe bananas
    (about 3 medium)
1½ cups all-purpose flour
1 teaspoon baking powder
1 teaspoon baking soda
½ teaspoon salt
¼ cup baking cocoa

1. Preheat oven to 350°. In a large bowl, cream butter and sugar until light and fluffy. Beat in egg and vanilla. Stir in mashed bananas. Combine flour, baking powder, baking soda and salt; add to the creamed mixture and mix well.

2. Divide the batter in half. Add cocoa to half; spread into a greased 13x9-in. baking pan. Spoon the remaining batter on top. If desired, swirl with a knife to marble batter.

3. Bake 25 minutes or until a toothpick inserted in the center comes out clean. Cool on a wire rack.

NUTRITION FACTS 2 bars: 181 cal., 7g fat (4g sat. fat), 31mg chol., 256mg sod., 29g carb. (17g sugars, 1g fiber), 2g pro.

DID YOU KNOW?

Mashed banana can be frozen for later. Mash the bananas with 1 teaspoon of lemon juice for each banana used. Freeze in 1- or 2-cup amounts in airtight containers for up to 6 months. When baking, about 1⅓ cups mashed bananas equals three medium or four small bananas.

Caramel Apple Bars

These bars make a great fall dessert. We like to warm individual servings in the microwave and serve them with a scoop of vanilla ice cream.

—CAROL STUBER OSAWATOMIE, KS

PREP: 25 MIN. • **BAKE:** 25 MIN.
MAKES: 20 BARS

CRUST
½ cup butter, softened
¼ cup shortening
1 cup packed brown sugar
1¾ cups all-purpose flour
1 cup old-fashioned or
   quick-cooking oats
1 teaspoon salt
½ teaspoon baking soda
½ cup chopped pecans, optional

FILLING
4½ cups coarsely chopped peeled
   tart apples
3 tablespoons all-purpose flour
1 package (14 ounces) caramels
3 tablespoons butter

1. Preheat oven to 400°. In a large bowl, cream butter, shortening and brown sugar until light and fluffy. Add flour, oats, salt and baking soda; mix well. If desired, stir in pecans. Set aside 2 cups of the oat mixture; press the remaining mixture into an ungreased 13x9-in. baking pan.

2. For filling, toss apples with flour; spoon over the crust. In a saucepan, melt the caramels and butter over low heat; drizzle over apples. Top with the reserved oat mixture.

3. Bake for 25-30 minutes or until lightly browned. Cool before cutting.

NUTRITION FACTS 1 bar: 267 cal., 11g fat (6g sat. fat), 18mg chol., 266mg sod., 42g carb. (27g sugars, 1g fiber), 3g pro.

Chunky Blond Brownies

Every bite of these chewy blond brownies is packed with chunks of white and semisweet chocolate and macadamia nuts.

—ROSEMARY DREISKE LEMMON, SD

PREP: 15 MIN. • **BAKE:** 25 MIN. + COOLING
MAKES: 2 DOZEN

½ cup butter, softened
¾ cup sugar
¾ cup packed brown sugar
2 large eggs
2 teaspoons vanilla extract
1½ cups all-purpose flour
1 teaspoon baking powder
½ teaspoon salt
1 cup white baking chips
1 cup semisweet chocolate chunks
1 jar (3 ounces) macadamia nuts or ¾ cup blanched almonds, chopped, divided

1. Preheat oven to 350°. In a large bowl, cream butter and sugars until light and fluffy. Beat in eggs and vanilla. Combine flour, baking powder and salt; gradually add to the creamed mixture and mix well. Stir in white chips, chocolate chunks and ½ cup of the nuts.

2. Spoon batter into a greased 13x9-in. baking pan; spread over the bottom of pan. The batter for this recipe is very thick, so be sure to spread it evenly. Sprinkle with the remaining nuts. Bake 25-30 minutes or until the top begins to crack and is golden brown. Cool on a wire rack. Cut into bars.

NUTRITION FACTS 1 brownie: 221 cal., 12g fat (6g sat. fat), 29mg chol., 130mg sod., 28g carb. (17g sugars, 1g fiber), 2g pro.

Pumpkin Pie Squares

This delicious dessert has all the spicy pumpkin goodness of the traditional pie without the fuss of a pastry crust.

—DENISE GOEDEKEN PLATTE CENTER, NE

PREP: 15 MIN.
BAKE: 1 HOUR 20 MIN. + COOLING
MAKES: 20 SQUARES

- 1 cup all-purpose flour
- ½ cup quick-cooking oats
- ½ cup packed brown sugar
- ½ cup cold butter

FILLING

- 2 cans (15 ounces each) solid-pack pumpkin
- 2 cans (12 ounces each) evaporated milk
- 4 large eggs
- 1½ cups granulated sugar
- 2 teaspoons ground cinnamon
- 1 teaspoon ground ginger
- ½ teaspoon ground cloves
- 1 teaspoon salt

TOPPING

- ½ cup packed brown sugar
- ½ cup chopped pecans
- 2 tablespoons butter, softened
  Sweetened whipped cream, optional

1. Preheat oven to 350°. Combine flour, oats and brown sugar. Cut in the butter until the mixture is crumbly. Press into a greased 13x9-in. pan. Bake until golden brown, about 20 minutes.

2. Meanwhile, beat the filling ingredients until smooth. Pour filling over the crust. Bake 45 minutes.

3. Combine the topping ingredients; sprinkle over the filling. Bake until a knife inserted in the center comes out clean, 15-20 minutes longer. Cool, then refrigerate until serving. If desired, serve with whipped cream.

NUTRITION FACTS 1 square: 248 cal., 10g fat (5g sat. fat), 64mg chol., 212mg sod., 36g carb. (28g sugars, 2g fiber), 4g pro.

Glazed Apple-Maple Blondies

My 6-year-old son and I conjured up this recipe to use the last of the apples we'd picked at the local orchard. For an extra treat, serve them warm with a dollop of sweetened whipped cream.
—HEATHER BATES ATHENS, ME

PREP: 25 MIN. • **BAKE:** 25 MIN. + COOLING
MAKES: 2 DOZEN

1⅓ cups packed brown sugar
½ cup butter, melted and cooled
½ cup maple syrup
2 teaspoons vanilla extract
2 large eggs
2 cups all-purpose flour
¾ teaspoon salt
¼ teaspoon baking soda
3 cups chopped peeled apples
 (about 3 medium)

GLAZE
¼ cup butter, cubed
½ cup maple syrup
¼ cup packed brown sugar

1. Preheat oven to 350°. Line a 13x9-in. baking pan with parchment paper, letting the ends extend up the sides of the pan.

2. In a large bowl, beat brown sugar, melted butter, maple syrup and vanilla until blended. Beat in eggs. In another bowl, whisk flour, salt and baking soda; gradually beat into the brown sugar mixture. Stir in apples (the batter will be thick).

3. Transfer batter to prepared pan. Bake 25-30 minutes or until golden brown and a toothpick inserted in center comes out with moist crumbs.

4. Meanwhile, in a small saucepan, melt butter over medium-low heat; stir in syrup and brown sugar. Bring to a boil over medium heat; cook and stir for 2-3 minutes or until slightly thickened. Remove from heat; cool slightly.

5. Pour the glaze over the warm blondies. Cool completely in pan on a wire rack. Cut into bars.

NUTRITION FACTS 1 blondie: 192 cal., 6g fat (4g sat. fat), 31mg chol., 149mg sod., 33g carb. (25g sugars, 0 fiber), 2g pro.

Chewy Pecan Pie Bars

I've been making these bars for many years—it's one of my husband's favorite recipes. The one-bowl preparation makes it quick and easy, with no mess—and the results are delicious!

—JUDY TAYLOR SHREVEPORT, LA

PREP: 10 MIN. • **BAKE:** 30 MIN. + COOLING
MAKES: 2 DOZEN

¼ cup butter, melted
2 cups packed brown sugar
⅔ cup all-purpose flour
4 large eggs
2 teaspoons vanilla extract
¼ teaspoon baking soda
¼ teaspoon salt
2 cups chopped pecans
   Confectioners' sugar, optional

1. Preheat oven to 350°. Pour melted butter into a 13x9-in. baking pan. In a large bowl, combine next six ingredients; mix well. Stir in pecans. Spread over the butter.

2. Bake 30-35 minutes. Remove from oven. If desired, immediately dust with confectioners' sugar. Cool before cutting.

NUTRITION FACTS 1 bar: 180 cal., 10g fat (2g sat. fat), 41mg chol., 75mg sod., 22g carb. (18g sugars, 1g fiber), 2g pro.

Fudge-Topped Brownies

Why choose between brownies and fudge when you can have both, all in one? These exquisite brownies are the ultimate chocolate dessert.

—**JUDY OLSON** WHITECOURT, AB

PREP: 25 MIN. • **BAKE:** 25 MIN. + FREEZING
MAKES: 10 DOZEN

1   cup butter
4   ounces unsweetened chocolate, chopped
2   cups sugar
2   teaspoons vanilla extract
4   large eggs
1½ cups all-purpose flour
1   teaspoon baking powder
½   teaspoon salt
1   cup chopped walnuts

TOPPING

4½ cups sugar
1   can (12 ounces) evaporated milk
½   cup butter, cubed
1   package (12 ounces) semisweet chocolate chips
1   package (11½ ounces) milk chocolate chips
1   jar (7 ounces) marshmallow creme
2   teaspoons vanilla extract
2   cups chopped walnuts

1. Preheat oven to 350°. In a heavy saucepan or microwave, melt butter and chocolate; stir until smooth. Remove from heat; blend in sugar and vanilla. Add eggs; mix well. Combine flour, baking powder and salt; add to the chocolate mixture. Stir in walnuts. Pour into a greased 13x9-in. baking pan. Bake for 25-30 minutes or until the top springs back when lightly touched. Cool on a wire rack.

2. For topping, combine sugar, milk and butter in a large heavy saucepan; bring to a boil over medium heat. Reduce the heat; simmer, uncovered, for 5 minutes, stirring constantly. Remove from heat. Stir in chocolate chips, marshmallow creme and vanilla until smooth. Add chopped walnuts. Spread over the warm brownies. Freeze for 3 hours or until firm. Cut into 1-in. squares. Store in the refrigerator.

NUTRITION FACTS 1 brownie: 128 cal., 6g fat (3g sat. fat), 15mg chol., 46mg sod., 18g carb. (15g sugars, 0 fiber), 2g pro.

Cinnamon Bars

Ellie gave us the recipe for these cookies with cinnamon and walnuts. Drizzle with icing, and serve with coffee or tea.
—**DIANE MYERS** STAR, ID

PREP: 25 MIN. • **BAKE:** 10 MIN. + COOLING
MAKES: 3 DOZEN

1	cup sugar
¾	cup canola oil
¼	cup honey
1	large egg
2	cups all-purpose flour
1	teaspoon baking soda
1	teaspoon ground cinnamon
¼	teaspoon salt
1	cup chopped walnuts, toasted

GLAZE

1	cup confectioners' sugar
2	tablespoons mayonnaise
1	teaspoon vanilla extract
1	to 2 tablespoons water
	Additional toasted chopped walnuts, optional

1. Preheat oven to 350°. In a large bowl, beat sugar, oil, honey and egg until well blended. In another bowl, whisk flour, baking soda, cinnamon and salt; gradually beat into sugar mixture. Stir in walnuts.

2. Spread into a greased 15x10x1-in. baking pan. Bake 10-12 minutes or until golden brown (edges will puff up). Cool completely on a wire rack.

3. For glaze, in a small bowl, mix confectioners' sugar, mayonnaise, vanilla and enough water to reach the desired consistency; spread over the top of the bars. If desired, sprinkle with additional walnuts. Let stand until set. Cut into bars. Refrigerate leftovers.

NOTE To toast nuts, bake in a shallow pan in a 350° oven for 5-10 minutes or cook in a skillet over low heat until lightly browned, stirring occasionally.

NUTRITION FACTS 1 bar (calculated without additional walnuts): 138 cal., 8g fat (1g sat. fat), 5mg chol., 58mg sod., 17g carb. (11g sugars, 0 fiber), 1g pro.

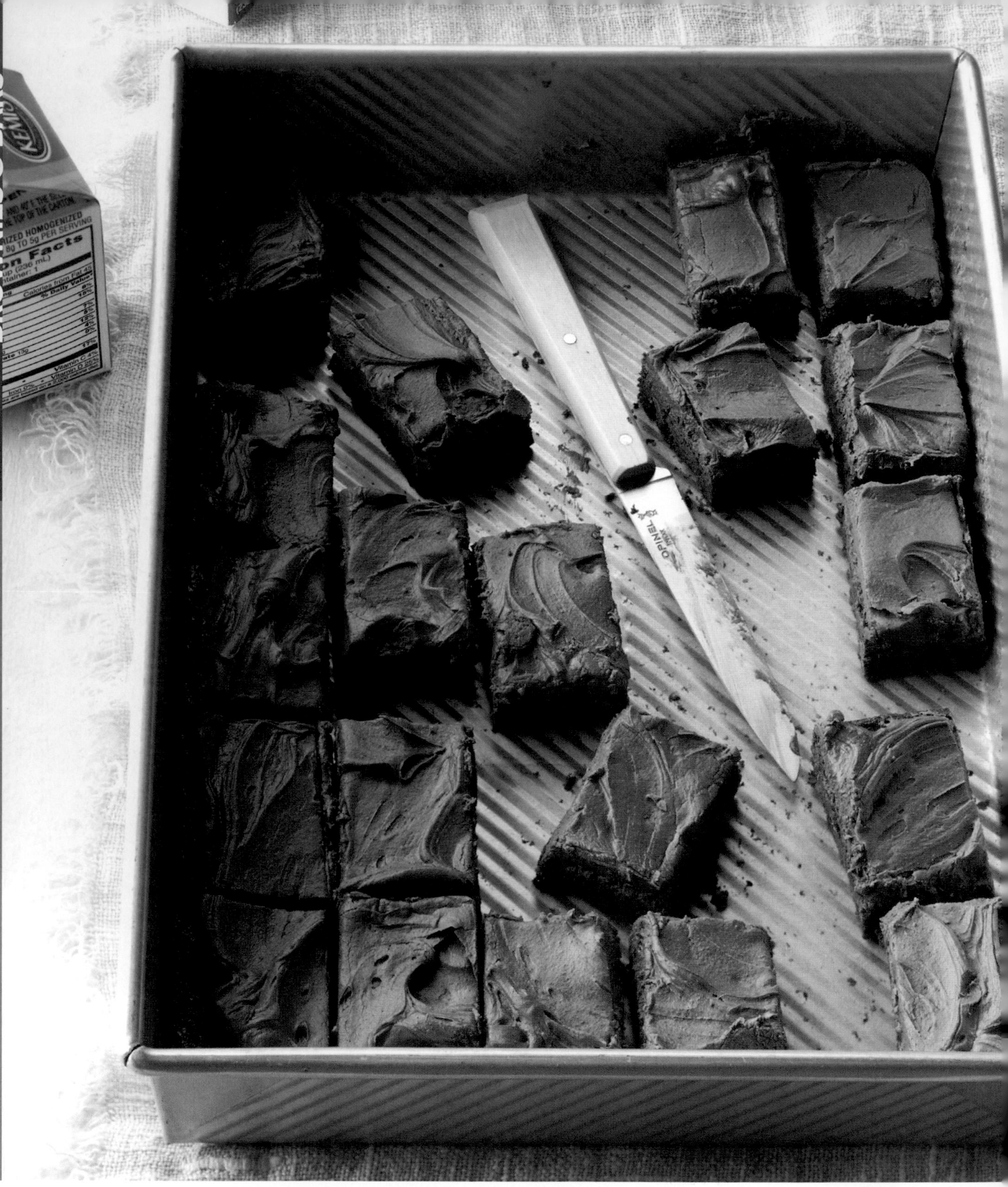

Cinnamon Brownies

For Christmas one year, a friend gave us a pan of these delicious brownies. Before I figured out their secret was cinnamon, half the pan was already gone!

—**GAIL MEHLE** ROCK SPRINGS, WY

PREP: 20 MIN. • **BAKE:** 30 MIN. + COOLING
MAKES: 3 DOZEN

- ¾ cup baking cocoa
- ½ teaspoon baking soda
- ⅔ cup butter, melted, divided
- ½ cup boiling water
- 2 cups sugar
- 2 large eggs, beaten
- 1 teaspoon vanilla extract
- 1⅓ cups all-purpose flour
- 1½ to 2 teaspoons ground cinnamon
- ¼ teaspoon salt
- 1 cup semisweet chocolate chips

FROSTING
- 6 tablespoons butter, softened
- ½ cup baking cocoa
- 2⅔ cups confectioners' sugar
- 1 to 1½ teaspoons ground cinnamon
- ⅓ cup evaporated milk
- 1 teaspoon vanilla extract

1. In a bowl, combine cocoa and baking soda; blend in ⅓ cup melted butter. Add boiling water, stirring until thickened. Stir in sugar, eggs, vanilla and remaining butter. Add flour, cinnamon and salt. Fold in chocolate chips. Pour into a greased 13x9-in. baking pan. Bake at 350° for 40 minutes or until the brownies test done. Cool.

2. For frosting, cream butter in a bowl. Combine cocoa, sugar and cinnamon; add alternately with milk. Beat to a spreading consistency; add vanilla. Add more milk if necessary, then spread over the brownies.

NUTRITION FACTS 1 brownie: 137 cal., 7g fat (4g sat. fat), 27mg chol., 94mg sod., 17g carb. (11g sugars, 1g fiber), 2g pro.

TOP TIP

The best thing we've found for cutting brownies and bars is a pizza cutter. It cuts smoothly and evenly through the brownie, producing less "drag" than a knife, and the chocolate doesn't stick to it.

Almond Blondies

Here's a sweet, sophisticated change from the typical chocolate brownie. When I bake these bites up, they don't last long.
—**CINDY PRUITT** GROVE, OK

PREP: 15 MIN. • **BAKE:** 25 MIN. + COOLING
MAKES: 16 BLONDIES

 2 large eggs
½ cup sugar
½ cup packed brown sugar
⅓ cup butter, melted
 1 teaspoon vanilla extract
¼ teaspoon almond extract
1⅓ cups all-purpose flour
½ teaspoon baking powder
¼ teaspoon salt
¼ cup chopped almonds

1. Preheat oven to 350°. In a large bowl, beat eggs, sugar and brown sugar for 3 minutes. Add butter and extracts; mix well. Combine flour, baking powder and salt. Gradually add to the creamed mixture, beating just until blended. Fold in almonds.

2. Pour batter into an 8-in. square baking pan coated with cooking spray. Bake for 25-30 minutes or until a toothpick inserted in the center comes out clean. Cool on a wire rack. Cut into squares.

NUTRITION FACTS 1 blondie: 143 cal., 6g fat (3g sat. fat), 36mg chol., 88mg sod., 21g carb. (13g sugars, 1g fiber), 2g pro. *Diabetic Exchanges:* 1½ starch, 1 fat.

Candy Bar Cheesecake Brownies

I came up with these brownies as a way to use my son's leftover Halloween candy. For a spooky touch, tint the cream cheese with orange food coloring!

—ELISABETH LARSEN PLEASANT GROVE, UT

PREP: 15 MIN. • **COOK:** 30 MIN. + CHILLING
MAKES: 2 DOZEN

- 1 cup butter, cubed
- 2 cups sugar
- 1/3 cup baking cocoa
- 2 teaspoons vanilla extract
- 4 large eggs
- 2 cups all-purpose flour
- 1 teaspoon salt
- 1 cup chopped assorted miniature candy bars (about 18)

TOPPING

- 1 package (8 ounces) cream cheese, softened
- 1/3 cup sugar
- 1/2 teaspoon vanilla extract
- 1 large egg
- 1/2 cup chopped assorted miniature candy bars (about 10)

1. Preheat oven to 350°. Grease a 13x9-in. baking pan. In a microwave, melt butter in a large microwave-safe bowl. Stir in sugar, cocoa and vanilla. Add eggs, one at a time, whisking to blend after each addition. Add flour and salt; stir just until combined. Stir in 1 cup candy bars. Spread batter into the prepared pan.

2. In a large bowl, beat cream cheese and sugar until smooth. Beat in vanilla. Add egg; beat on low speed just until blended. Drop by tablespoonfuls over the batter. Cut through batter with a knife to swirl. Sprinkle with 1/2 cup candy bars.

3. Bake for 30-35 minutes or until the filling in the center is almost set. Cool for around 1 hour in pan on a wire rack. Refrigerate for at least 2 hours. Cut into 24 bars.

NUTRITION FACTS 1 brownie: 282 cal., 14g fat (8g sat. fat), 71mg chol., 233mg sod., 36g carb. (25g sugars, 1g fiber), 4g pro.

Peach-Blueberry
Crumble Tart, p. 148

CHAPTER 6

PIES & TARTS

Home-baked pies dress up in rich harvest flavors in the fall.

Ginger Plum Tart

Sweet cravings, begone: This free-form plum tart is done in only 35 minutes! Plus, it's super delicious when served warm.

—*TASTE OF HOME* TEST KITCHEN

PREP: 15 MIN. • **BAKE:** 20 MIN. + COOLING
MAKES: 8 SERVINGS

1	sheet refrigerated pie pastry
3½	cups sliced fresh plums (about 10 medium)
3	tablespoons plus 1 teaspoon coarse sugar, divided
1	tablespoon cornstarch
2	teaspoons finely chopped crystallized ginger
1	large egg white
1	tablespoon water

1. Preheat oven to 400°. On a work surface, unroll pastry sheet. Roll to a 12-in. circle. Transfer to a parchment paper-lined baking sheet.

2. In a large bowl, toss plums with 3 tablespoons of the sugar and the cornstarch. Arrange the plums on the pastry to within 2 in. of edges; sprinkle with ginger. Fold the pastry edge over the plums in rustic pleats.

3. In a small bowl, whisk egg white and water; brush over the folded pastry. Sprinkle with the remaining sugar.

4. Bake 20-25 minutes or until the crust is golden brown. Cool on pan on a wire rack. Serve warm or at room temperature.

NUTRITION FACTS 1 slice: 190 cal., 7g fat (3g sat. fat), 5mg chol., 108mg sod., 30g carb. (14g sugars, 1g fiber), 2g pro. *Diabetic Exchanges:* 1½ starch, 1 fat, ½ fruit.

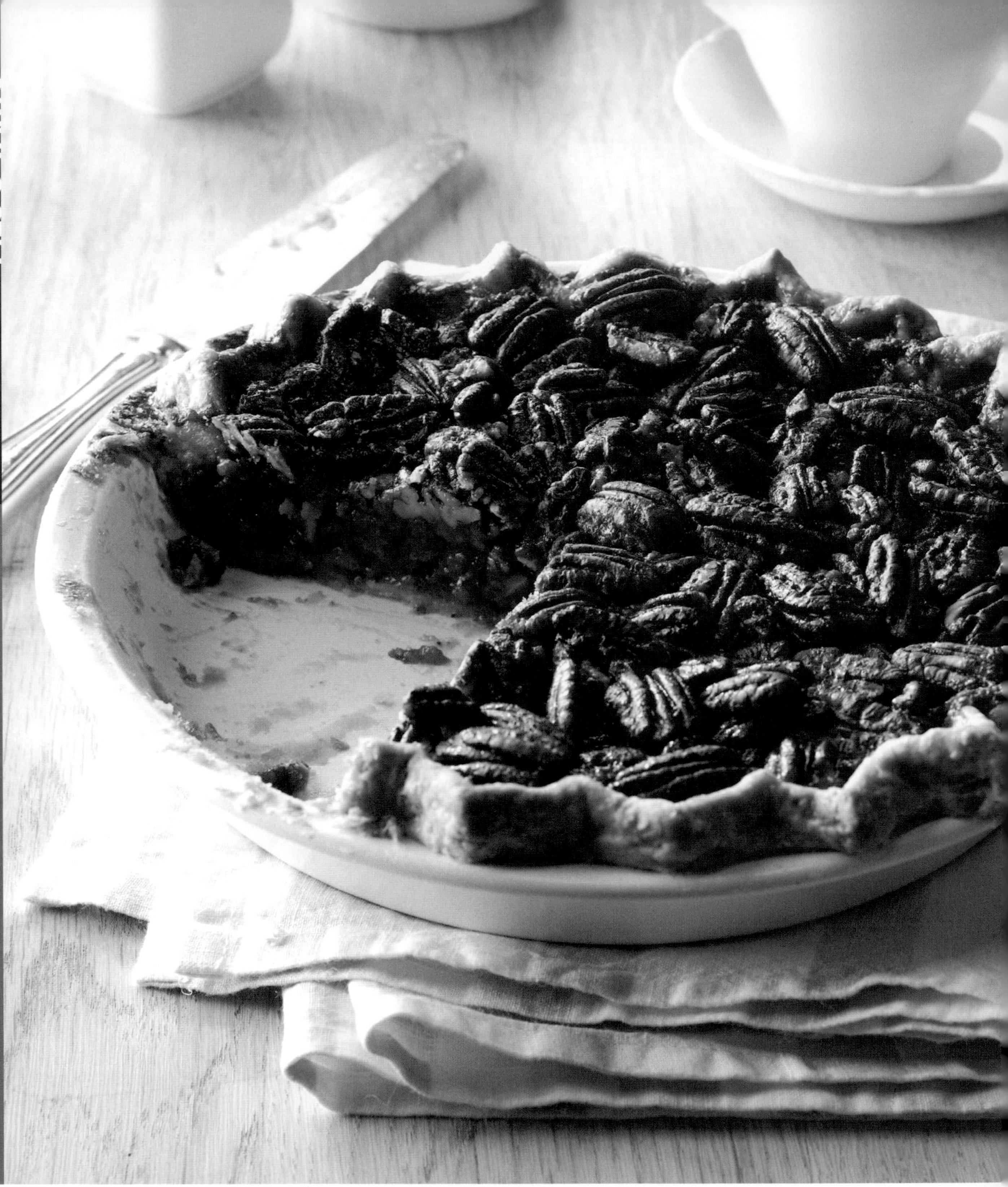

Honey Pecan Pie

Looking for a grand finale for a special meal? This attractive pecan pie is bound to please with its traditional filling topped with honey-glazed pecans.

—**CATHY HUDAK** WADSWORTH, OH

PREP: 25 MIN. • **BAKE:** 45 MIN. + COOLING
MAKES: 8 SERVINGS

- 4 large eggs
- 1 cup chopped pecans
- 1 cup light corn syrup
- ¼ cup sugar
- ¼ cup packed brown sugar
- 2 tablespoons butter, melted
- 1 teaspoon vanilla extract
- ½ teaspoon salt
- 1 pastry shell (9 inches), unbaked

TOPPING
- 3 tablespoons butter
- ⅓ cup packed brown sugar
- 3 tablespoons honey
- 1½ cups pecan halves

1. Preheat oven to 350°. In a large bowl, combine eggs, pecans, corn syrup, sugars, butter, vanilla and salt. Pour into pastry shell. Bake for 30 minutes.

2. In a small saucepan, melt butter over medium heat. Stir in brown sugar and honey until combined. Stir in pecan halves until coated. Spoon over the pie.

3. Bake 15-20 minutes longer or until a knife inserted in the center comes out clean. Cool completely on a wire rack. Refrigerate leftovers.

NUTRITION FACTS 1 slice: 688 cal., 42g fat (10g sat. fat), 130mg chol., 408mg sod., 78g carb. (52g sugars, 3g fiber), 7g pro.

DID YOU KNOW?

A "transparent" pie is one with a glossy sweet filling based on brown sugar, molasses, corn or maple syrup. Pecan pie is a classic example. Typically thickened with egg, these pies can include tart jellies, lemon or vinegar to cut the sweetness. Cream, butter, spices, nuts or dried fruits are often added as well.

Figgy Apple Brie Tart

Our family holiday gatherings often included baked brie.
I transformed it into a dessert that's both savory and sweet.
—**KRISTIE SCHLEY** SEVERNA PARK, MD

PREP: 25 MIN. • **BAKE:** 15 MIN. + COOLING
MAKES: 8 SERVINGS

- 3 tablespoons butter, softened
- ¾ cup sugar
- 2 large apples
- 1 cup dried figs, halved
- ½ pound Brie cheese, rind removed, sliced
- 1 sheet refrigerated pie pastry

1. Preheat oven to 425°. Spread butter over bottom of a 10-in. ovenproof skillet; sprinkle evenly with sugar.

2. Peel, quarter and core apples; arrange in a circular pattern over the sugar, rounded side down. Place figs around the apples. Place the skillet over medium heat; cook 10-12 minutes or until the sugar is caramelized and the apples have softened slightly. Remove from heat; top with cheese.

3. Unroll pastry sheet; place over the apples, tucking the edges under. Place the skillet in the oven on an upper rack; bake 15-18 minutes or until the crust is golden brown. Cool in skillet 5 minutes. Carefully invert onto a serving plate; serve warm.

NUTRITION FACTS 1 slice: 394 cal., 19g fat (11g sat. fat), 45mg chol., 315mg sod., 50g carb. (33g sugars, 2g fiber), 8g pro.

PIES & TARTS

Dark Chocolate Truffle Tart

Espresso intensifies the dark chocolate flavor of my truffle tart. I make the crust with toasted walnuts and dust the cooled dessert with baking cocoa before serving.

—**JOHNNA JOHNSON** SCOTTSDALE, AZ

PREP: 20 MIN. + CHILLING
BAKE: 20 MIN. + COOLING
MAKES: 12 SERVINGS

⅓	cup walnut halves, toasted
⅓	cup confectioners' sugar
½	cup all-purpose flour
3	tablespoons baking cocoa
⅛	teaspoon salt
⅓	cup cold unsalted butter, cubed

FILLING

8	ounces semisweet chocolate, chopped
¼	cup unsalted butter
⅔	cup heavy whipping cream
1¼	teaspoons instant espresso powder
2	large eggs, lightly beaten
1	large egg yolk
⅓	cup sugar
1½	teaspoons vanilla extract
	Additional baking cocoa

1. Place walnuts and confectioners' sugar in a food processor; pulse until the walnuts are finely chopped. Add flour, cocoa and salt; pulse until blended. Add butter; pulse until the mixture resembles coarse crumbs.

2. Preheat oven to 350°. Press dough onto bottom and up the sides of a greased 9-in. fluted tart pan with a removable bottom. Refrigerate for 30 minutes. Bake 10 minutes.

3. Meanwhile, for filling, in a double boiler or metal bowl over hot water, melt chocolate and butter; stir until smooth. Stir in cream and espresso powder. Remove from heat; cool slightly. Whisk in eggs, egg yolk, sugar and vanilla.

4. Pour the filling into the warm crust. Bake for 20-25 minutes or until the center is just set (the mixture will jiggle). Cool completely on a wire rack. Dust with cocoa before serving.

NUTRITION FACTS 1 slice: 326 cal., 24g fat (13g sat. fat), 85mg chol., 42mg sod., 19g carb. (13g sugars, 1g fiber), 4g pro.

Raisin Pecan Pie

I remember my Grandmother Voltie and Great-Aunt Ophelia making this southern-style pie for Thanksgiving. It was always one of the many delicious cakes and pies lined up for dessert.
—**ANGIE PRICE** BRADFORD, TN

PREP: 20 MIN. + CHILLING
BAKE: 35 MIN. + COOLING
MAKES: 8 SERVINGS

Pastry for single-crust pie (9 inches)
½ cup boiling water
½ cup golden raisins
3 large eggs
1½ cups sugar
½ cup butter, melted
2 teaspoons cider vinegar
1 teaspoon vanilla extract
½ teaspoon ground cinnamon
½ teaspoon ground cloves
¼ teaspoon ground nutmeg
½ cup chopped pecans

1. Preheat oven to 350°. On a lightly floured surface, roll pastry dough to a ⅛-in.-thick circle; transfer to a 9-in. pie plate. Trim the pastry to ½ in. beyond the rim of the plate; flute the edge. Refrigerate for 30 minutes.

2. Pour boiling water over raisins in a small bowl; let stand 5 minutes. Drain. In a large bowl, beat eggs, sugar, melted butter, vinegar, vanilla and spices until blended. Stir in pecans and the drained raisins. Pour into the pastry shell.

3. Bake on a lower oven rack 35-40 minutes or until the filling is set. Cool on a wire rack. Refrigerate leftovers.

PASTRY FOR SINGLE-CRUST PIE (9 INCHES) Combine 1¼ cups all-purpose flour and ¼ teaspoon salt; cut in ½ cup cold butter until crumbly. Gradually add 3-5 tablespoons ice water, tossing with a fork until dough holds together when pressed. Wrap in plastic wrap and refrigerate 1 hour.

NUTRITION FACTS 1 slice: 524 cal., 30g fat (16g sat. fat), 130mg chol., 275mg sod., 61g carb. (44g sugars, 2g fiber), 6g pro.

Scrumptious Sweet Potato Pie

This sweet potato pie is distinctive because it doesn't contain milk. It does have a splash of whiskey and a hint of lemon, however!

—SUZANNE SMITH MAUMEE, OH

PREP: 1 HOUR + CHILLING
BAKE: 40 MIN. + COOLING
MAKES: 8 SERVINGS

    Pastry for single-crust pie (9 inches)
1½ pounds sweet potatoes (about
    2 medium), peeled and cubed
⅓ cup butter, softened
⅔ cup sugar
¼ teaspoon ground cinnamon
⅛ teaspoon ground nutmeg
⅛ teaspoon baking powder
 2 large eggs, lightly beaten
 1 teaspoon vanilla extract
¼ teaspoon lemon extract
 1 to 2 tablespoons whiskey or
    apple juice

1. On a lightly floured surface, roll pastry dough to a ⅛-in.-thick circle; transfer to a 9-in. pie plate. Trim the pastry to ½ in. beyond the rim of the plate; flute the edge. Refrigerate for 30 minutes. Preheat oven to 425°.

2. Place the sweet potatoes in a large saucepan; add enough water to cover. Bring to a boil over high heat. Reduce heat to medium; cook, uncovered, for 15-18 minutes or until tender. Drain well; return to pot. Mash potatoes until smooth (you should have 2 cups).

3. Line the pastry with a double thickness of foil. Fill with pie weights, dried beans or uncooked rice. Bake on a lower oven rack for 15-20 minutes or until the edges are light golden brown. Remove foil and weights; bake 3-6 minutes longer or until the bottom is golden brown. Cool on a wire rack. Reduce oven to 350°.

4. Beat butter, sugar, cinnamon, nutmeg and baking powder until blended. Beat in the eggs, sweet potatoes and extracts until smooth. Stir in whiskey.

5. Add the filling to the crust. Bake on a middle rack 40-45 minutes or until the center is set. Cool on a wire rack; serve or refrigerate within 2 hours.

PASTRY FOR SINGLE-CRUST PIE (9 INCHES) Combine 1¼ cups all-purpose flour and ¼ teaspoon salt; cut in ½ cup cold butter until crumbly. Gradually add 3-5 tablespoons ice water, tossing with a fork until dough holds together when pressed. Wrap in plastic wrap and refrigerate 1 hour.

NUTRITION FACTS 1 piece: 413 cal., 21g fat (13g sat. fat), 97mg chol., 248mg sod., 53g carb. (26g sugars, 3g fiber), 5g pro.

Best Lime Tart

This treat is the perfect balance between tart and sweet, and the almonds in the crust are just wonderful. This is one of my husband's favorite desserts.

—CHARIS O'CONNELL MOHNTON, PA

PREP: 35 MIN. • **BAKE:** 15 MIN. + CHILLING
MAKES: 12 SERVINGS

1¼ cups graham cracker crumbs
5 tablespoons butter, melted
¼ cup ground almonds
3 tablespoons sugar
FILLING
4 large egg yolks
1 can (14 ounces) sweetened condensed milk
½ cup lime juice
2 teaspoons grated lime peel
TOPPING
½ cup heavy whipping cream
1 tablespoon sugar
½ cup sour cream
1 teaspoon grated lime peel
Fresh raspberries and lime wedges

1. Preheat oven to 325°. In a small bowl, combine cracker crumbs, butter, almonds and sugar. Press onto the bottom and up the sides of a greased 9-in. tart pan. Bake for 15-18 minutes or until the edges are lightly browned.

2. In a large bowl, whisk egg yolks, milk, lime juice and peel. Pour over the crust. Bake for 12-14 minutes or until the center is almost set. Cool on a wire rack. Refrigerate for at least 2 hours.

3. In a large bowl, beat cream until it begins to thicken. Add sugar; beat until stiff peaks form. Fold in sour cream and grated lime peel. Spread over the tart. Garnish with fresh raspberries and lime wedges.

NUTRITION FACTS 1 slice: 288 cal., 16g fat (9g sat. fat), 112mg chol., 138mg sod., 31g carb. (26g sugars, 1g fiber), 5g pro.

PIES & TARTS

Cranberry-Almond Apple Pie

This recipe is a family treasure. My grandmother baked her special pie every year for Christmas. It's so much better than everyday apple pie!

—**MAXINE THERIAUIT** NASHUA, NH

PREP: 15 MIN. • **BAKE:** 1 HOUR
MAKES: 8 SERVINGS

---

1   cup sugar
¼   cup all-purpose flour
3   tablespoons butter, melted
½   teaspoon ground nutmeg
⅛   teaspoon salt
6   medium tart apples, peeled and thinly sliced
1   cup fresh or frozen cranberries
1   pastry shell (9 inches), unbaked

TOPPING
½   cup packed brown sugar
⅓   cup all-purpose flour
½   teaspoon ground cinnamon
3   tablespoons cold butter
⅓   cup sliced almonds, toasted

1. Preheat oven to 350°. In a bowl, combine sugar, flour, butter, nutmeg and salt. Add apples and cranberries; stir gently. Pour into pastry shell.

2. In a small bowl, combine brown sugar, flour and cinnamon; cut in butter until crumbly. Stir in almonds; sprinkle over the filling. Bake for 1 hour or until the apples are tender.

NUTRITION FACTS 1 slice: 453 cal., 18g fat (9g sat. fat), 28mg chol., 230mg sod., 73g carb. (50g sugars, 3g fiber), 3g pro.

TOP TIP

To freeze fresh cranberries, place them in a single layer on a 13x9-in. baking pan in the freezer until frozen, then transfer them to an airtight container and freeze for up to 1 year. Before using, wash the berries and pluck off any stems. There's no need to thaw frozen cranberries before using them in recipes.

Peach-Blueberry Crumble Tart

Easy to prepare, this fruity tart is a favorite in our family, whether served fresh out of the oven or at room temperature with a scoop of vanilla ice cream.

—JAMES SCHEND PLEASANT PRAIRIE, WI

PREP: 30 MIN. + COOLING • **BAKE:** 35 MIN.
MAKES: 12 SERVINGS

1⅓ cups all-purpose flour
¼ cup sugar
¼ teaspoon ground cinnamon
½ cup butter, melted
2 cups frozen unsweetened blueberries, thawed
2 cups frozen unsweetened sliced peaches, thawed
1 tablespoon honey

CRUMB TOPPING

¼ cup all-purpose flour
¼ cup packed brown sugar
¼ cup old-fashioned oats
¼ cup chopped pecans
⅛ teaspoon ground cloves
2 tablespoons butter, melted

1. Preheat oven to 350°. In a small bowl, mix flour, sugar and cinnamon; stir in butter just until blended. Press onto the bottom and up the sides of a 9-in. fluted tart pan with removable bottom. Bake for 15-20 minutes or until lightly browned. Cool on a wire rack.

2. In a large bowl, combine blueberries, peaches and honey; toss to coat. In a small bowl, combine the first five topping ingredients; stir in butter.

3. Spoon the fruit mixture into the crust; sprinkle with the topping. Bake for 35-40 minutes or until the topping is golden brown and the filling is bubbly. Cool on a wire rack at least 15 minutes before serving.

NUTRITION FACTS 1 slice: 229 cal., 12g fat (6g sat. fat), 25mg chol., 70mg sod., 30g carb. (15g sugars, 2g fiber), 3g pro.

DID YOU KNOW?

Quick-cooking and old-fashioned oats can be interchanged in baked goods, but old-fashioned oats add more texture, so you may notice a difference. Steel-cut oats are tougher and require longer cooking times, so are not usually recommended for baking.

Almond Pear Tart

I had never seen a pie without a pan until my daughter brought back this delectable recipe from an exchange program in Belgium. It's still a family favorite after all these years.

—**C. B. (SHERRY) LAMAY** CAPITAN, NM

PREP: 15 MIN. • **BAKE:** 20 MIN. + COOLING
MAKES: 8 SERVINGS

    Pastry for single-crust pie (9 inches)
- ¾ cup plus 2 teaspoons sugar, divided
- 3 tablespoons all-purpose flour
- 4 cups sliced peeled fresh pears (about 4 medium)
- 3 tablespoons sliced almonds

1. Preheat oven to 450°. On a lightly floured surface, roll pastry into a 10-in. circle. Transfer to a parchment paper-lined baking sheet.

2. In a large bowl, combine ¾ cup sugar and flour; add pears and toss to coat. Spoon over the pastry to within 2 in. of edges. Fold up edges of pastry over filling, leaving center uncovered. Sprinkle with remaining sugar.

3. Bake for 15 minutes or until the crust is golden and filling is bubbly. Sprinkle with almonds; bake 5 minutes longer. Using the parchment paper, slide tart onto a wire rack to cool.

PASTRY FOR SINGLE-CRUST PIE (9 INCHES) Combine 1¼ cups all-purpose flour and ¼ teaspoon salt; cut in ½ cup cold butter until crumbly. Gradually add 3-5 tablespoons ice water, tossing with a fork until dough holds together when pressed. Wrap in plastic wrap and refrigerate 1 hour.

NUTRITION FACTS 1 slice: 269 cal., 8g fat (3g sat. fat), 5mg chol., 100mg sod., 48g carb. (29g sugars, 2g fiber), 2g pro.

Cranberry Cheese Crumb Pie

My mind works overtime to plan special desserts to surprise the family. When friends come to share this cranberry pie, everyone gives it a *wow*.

—LORRAINE CALAND SHUNIAH, ON

PREP: 20 MIN. • **BAKE:** 45 MIN. + CHILLING
MAKES: 10 SERVINGS

- 1   sheet refrigerated pie pastry
- 8   ounces cream cheese, softened
- 1   can (14 ounces) sweetened condensed milk
- ¼   cup lemon juice

CRANBERRY LAYER

- 1   can (14 ounces) whole-berry cranberry sauce
- 2   tablespoons cornstarch
- 1   tablespoon brown sugar

TOPPING

- ½   cup all-purpose flour
- ¼   cup packed brown sugar
- ½   teaspoon ground cinnamon
- ¼   cup cold butter, cubed
- ¾   cup chopped pecans

1. Preheat oven to 375°. Unroll the pastry sheet into a 9-in. pie plate; flute edge. In a small bowl, beat cream cheese, milk and lemon juice until smooth. Spread evenly into the crust.

2. In a small bowl, mix the cranberry layer ingredients; spoon over the cream cheese mixture. For the topping, in another bowl, mix flour, brown sugar and cinnamon; cut in butter until crumbly. Stir in pecans. Sprinkle over the cranberry layer.

3. Bake 45-55 minutes or until the crust and topping are golden brown. Cover the edge loosely with foil during the last 10 minutes if needed to prevent overbrowning. Remove foil. Cool for 1 hour on a wire rack; refrigerate at least 2 hours before serving.

NUTRITION FACTS 1 slice: 512 cal., 27g fat (12g sat. fat), 55mg chol., 260mg sod., 62g carb. (40g sugars, 2g fiber), 7g pro.

Farm Apple Pan Pie

Pick this pie for convenient carrying to your next covered-dish supper, potluck or picnic. But be prepared—people always ask for the recipe!

—DOLORES SKROUT SUMMERHILL, PA

PREP: 30 MIN. • **BAKE:** 50 MIN.
MAKES: 24 SERVINGS

EGG YOLK PASTRY

- 5 cups all-purpose flour
- 4 teaspoons sugar
- ½ teaspoon salt
- ½ teaspoon baking powder
- 1½ cups shortening
- 2 large egg yolks, lightly beaten
- ¾ cup cold water

FILLING

- 5 pounds tart apples, peeled and thinly sliced
- 4 teaspoons lemon juice
- ¾ cup sugar
- ¾ cup packed brown sugar
- 1 teaspoon ground cinnamon
- ½ teaspoon ground nutmeg
- ¼ teaspoon salt
  Whole milk
  Additional sugar

1. In a large bowl, combine flour, sugar, salt and baking powder; cut in shortening until the mixture resembles coarse crumbs. Combine egg yolks and cold water. Sprinkle over the dry ingredients; toss with fork. If needed, add additional water, 1 tablespoon at a time, until the mixture can be formed into a ball.

2. Divide the dough in half. On a lightly floured surface, roll half of the dough to fit a 15x10x1-in. baking pan.

3. Sprinkle apples with lemon juice; arrange half of them over the dough. Combine the sugars, cinnamon, nutmeg and salt; sprinkle half over the apples. Top with the remaining apples; sprinkle with the remaining sugar mixture.

4. Roll the remaining pastry to fit the pan; place on top of the filling and seal the edges. Brush with milk and sprinkle with sugar. Cut vents in the top pastry. Bake at 400° for 50 minutes or until the crust is golden brown and the filling is bubbly.

NUTRITION FACTS 1 piece: 317 cal., 13g fat (3g sat. fat), 18mg chol., 86mg sod., 48g carb. (26g sugars, 3g fiber), 3g pro.

Blueberry Buckle, p. 162

CHAPTER 7

COBBLERS, CRISPS & MORE

Served warm with ice cream, these classic desserts define comfort food.

Rhubarb Mandarin Crisp

An attractive and distinctive dessert, this crisp is also a popular breakfast dish at our house, served with a glass of milk rather than topped with ice cream. Since it calls for lots of rhubarb, it's a great use for the bounty you harvest.

—**RACHAEL VANDENDOOL** BARRY'S BAY, ON

PREP: 20 MIN. + STANDING • **BAKE:** 40 MIN.
MAKES: 12 SERVINGS

- 6 cups chopped fresh or frozen rhubarb
- 1½ cups sugar
- 5 tablespoons quick-cooking tapioca
- 1 can (11 ounces) mandarin oranges, drained
- 1 cup packed brown sugar
- 1 cup quick-cooking oats
- ½ cup all-purpose flour
- ½ teaspoon salt
- ½ cup cold butter, cubed
  Ice cream, optional

1. Preheat oven to 350°. In a large bowl, toss rhubarb, sugar and tapioca; let stand for 15 minutes, stirring occasionally. Pour into a greased 13x9-in. baking pan. Top with oranges.

2. In a large bowl, combine brown sugar, oats, flour and salt. Cut in butter until the mixture resembles coarse crumbs; sprinkle evenly over the oranges.

3. Bake for 40 minutes or until the top is golden brown. If desired, serve with ice cream.

NOTE If using frozen rhubarb, measure the rhubarb while still frozen, then thaw completely. Drain rhubarb in a colander, but do not press out the liquid.

NUTRITION FACTS 1 serving (calculated without ice cream): 323 cal., 8g fat (5g sat. fat), 20mg chol., 187mg sod., 62g carb. (48g sugars, 2g fiber), 2g pro.

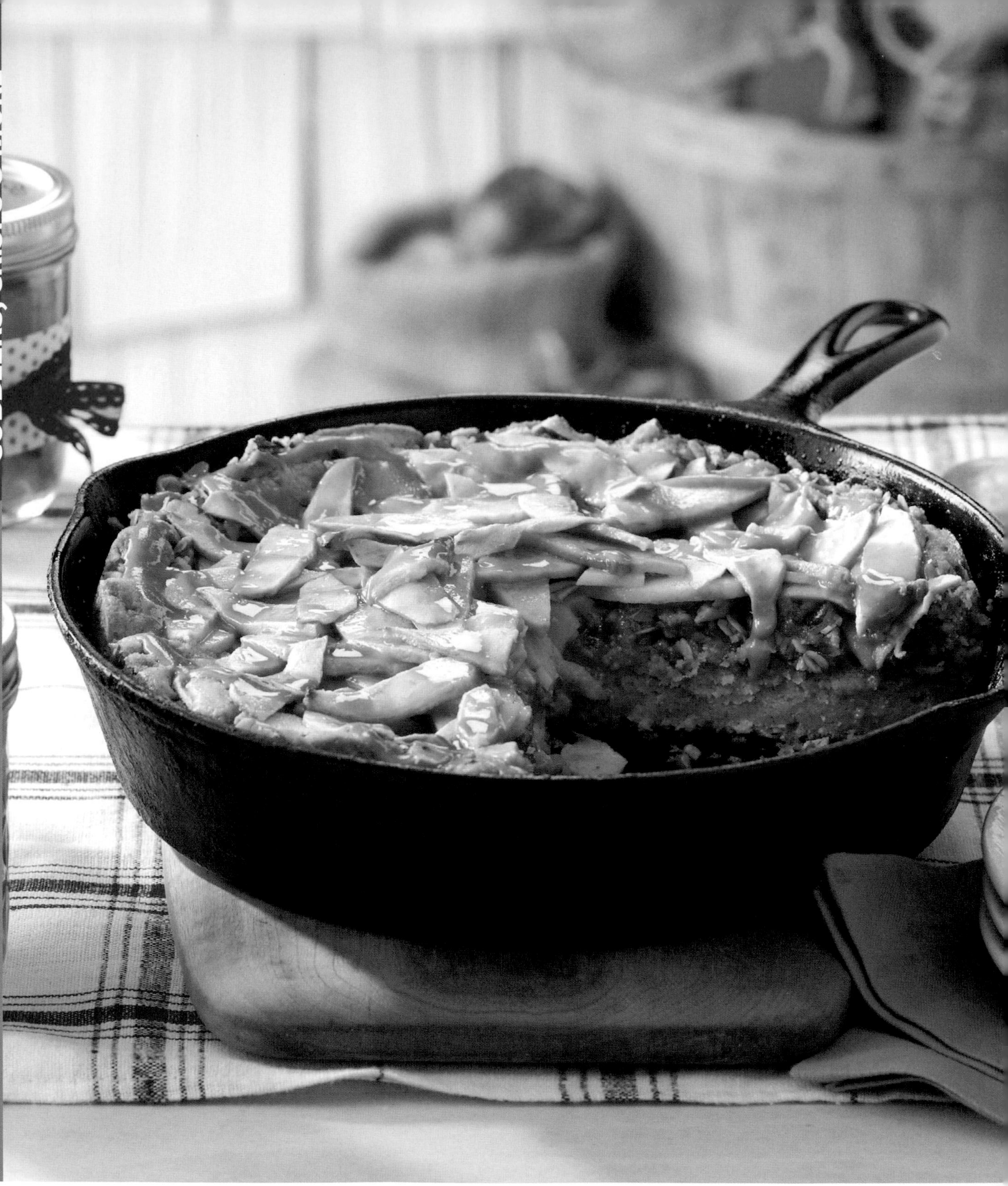

Caramel-Apple Skillet Buckle

My grandma made a version of this for me when I was a little girl. She used fresh apples from a tree in the backyard. I've adapted her recipe to include pecans and caramel with the fruit because I love the combination.

—EMILY HOBBS SPRINGFIELD, MO

PREP: 35 MIN.
BAKE: 1 HOUR + STANDING
MAKES: 12 SERVINGS

½ cup butter, softened
¾ cup sugar
2 large eggs
1 teaspoon vanilla extract
2 cups all-purpose flour
2½ teaspoons baking powder
1¾ teaspoons ground cinnamon
½ teaspoon ground ginger
¼ teaspoon salt
1½ cups buttermilk

TOPPING
⅔ cup packed brown sugar
½ cup all-purpose flour
¼ cup cold butter
¾ cup finely chopped pecans
½ cup old-fashioned oats
6 cups thinly sliced peeled
   Gala or other sweet apples
   (about 6 medium)
18 caramels, unwrapped
1 tablespoon buttermilk
   Vanilla ice cream, optional

1. Preheat oven to 350°. In a large bowl, cream butter and sugar until light and fluffy. Add eggs, one at a time, beating well after each addition. Beat in vanilla. In another bowl, whisk flour, baking powder, cinnamon, ginger and salt; add to creamed mixture alternately with buttermilk, beating well after each addition. Pour into a greased 12-in. ovenproof skillet.

2. For the topping, in a small bowl, mix brown sugar and flour; cut in butter until crumbly. Stir in pecans and oats; sprinkle over the batter. Top with apples. Bake 60-70 minutes or until the apples are golden brown. Cool in pan on a wire rack.

3. In a microwave, melt caramels with buttermilk; stir until smooth. Drizzle over the cake. Let stand until set. If desired, serve with ice cream.

NUTRITION FACTS 1 serving (calculated without ice cream): 462 cal., 19g fat (9g sat. fat), 64mg chol., 354mg sod., 68g carb. (42g sugars, 3g fiber), 7g pro.

Blueberry Buckle

Buckle is a family favorite, served warm at the end of a meal, either plain or with a scoop of ice cream. We also like it cold as a coffee cake. The lemon sauce makes this traditional dessert a little different, and it enhances the flavor of the blueberries.

—MAUREEN CARR CARMAN, MB

PREP: 20 MIN. • **BAKE:** 45 MIN.
MAKES: 9 SERVINGS (1 CUP SAUCE)

- 2 cups all-purpose flour
- 1/3 cup sugar
- 2 teaspoons baking powder
- 1/4 teaspoon salt
- 1 large egg
- 1/2 cup 2% milk
- 1/2 cup butter, melted
- 2 cups fresh or frozen blueberries, thawed

TOPPING
- 1/2 cup sugar
- 1/3 cup all-purpose flour
- 1/2 teaspoon ground cinnamon
- 1/4 cup cold butter, cubed

LEMON SAUCE
- 1/3 cup sugar
- 1 tablespoon cornstarch
- 1 teaspoon grated lemon peel
- 1 cup water
- 1 tablespoon butter
- 1 tablespoon lemon juice

1. Preheat oven to 350°. In a large bowl, combine flour, sugar, baking powder and salt. In a small bowl, whisk egg, milk and butter; add to the dry ingredients just until moistened. Spread batter into a greased 8-in. square baking dish. Top with blueberries.

2. For the topping, in a small bowl, combine sugar, flour and cinnamon; cut in butter until crumbly. Sprinkle over the blueberries.

3. Bake 45-55 minutes or until golden brown and a toothpick inserted in the center comes out clean.

4. For the sauce, in a small saucepan, combine sugar, cornstarch and lemon peel; gradually stir in water until smooth. Bring to a boil over low heat, stirring constantly. Cook and stir 1 minute longer or until thickened. Remove from heat; stir in butter and lemon juice. Serve warm with buckle.

NUTRITION FACTS 1 serving: 402 cal., 18g fat (11g sat. fat), 68mg chol., 285mg sod., 57g carb. (30g sugars, 2g fiber), 5g pro.

Macaroon Apple Cobbler

If your time is short, use apple pie filling instead of the fresh apples.

—PHYLLIS HINCK LAKE CITY, MN

PREP: 15 MIN. • **BAKE:** 25 MIN.
MAKES: 8 SERVINGS

---

  4 cups thinly sliced peeled tart apples
⅓ cup sugar
½ teaspoon ground cinnamon
½ cup flaked coconut
¼ cup chopped pecans
TOPPING
½ cup butter, softened
½ cup sugar
  1 large egg
½ teaspoon vanilla extract
¾ cup all-purpose flour
¼ teaspoon baking powder

1. Preheat oven to 350°. Place apples in an ungreased 9-in. pie plate. Combine sugar and cinnamon; sprinkle over the apples. Top with coconut and pecans; set aside.

2. To make the topping, cream butter and sugar until light and fluffy. Beat in egg and vanilla. Combine flour and baking powder; gradually add to the creamed mixture until blended.

3. Drop small spoonfuls of the batter over the apples. Bake for 25-35 minutes or until the top is golden brown and the fruit is tender. Serve warm.

NUTRITION FACTS 1 serving: 320 cal., 17g fat (9g sat. fat), 57mg chol., 152mg sod., 41g carb. (29g sugars, 2g fiber), 3g pro.

Chocolate Cobbler

Cobbler topping without the fruit! It's impossible to resist the flavorful chocolate sauce that appears like magic when this delightful cake bakes.

—MARGARET MCNEIL GERMANTOWN, TN

PREP: 10 MIN. • **BAKE:** 40 MIN.
MAKES: 8 SERVINGS

- 1 cup self-rising flour
- ½ cup sugar
- 2 tablespoons plus ¼ cup baking cocoa, divided
- ½ cup whole milk
- 3 tablespoons vegetable oil
- 1 cup packed brown sugar
- 1¾ cups hot water
  Vanilla ice cream, optional

Preheat oven to 350°. In a bowl, combine flour, sugar and 2 tablespoons cocoa. Stir in milk and oil until smooth. Pour into a greased 8-in. square baking pan. Combine brown sugar and the remaining cocoa; sprinkle over the batter. Pour hot water over the top (do not stir). Bake for 40-45 minutes or until top of cake springs back when lightly touched. If desired, serve warm with ice cream.

NOTE As a substitute for 1 cup of self-rising flour, place 1½ teaspoons baking powder and ½ teaspoon salt in a measuring cup. Add all-purpose flour to measure 1 cup.

NUTRITION FACTS 1 serving (calculated without ice cream): 267 cal., 6g fat (1g sat. fat), 2mg chol., 198mg sod., 53g carb. (40g sugars, 1g fiber), 3g pro.

Peach & Berry Bliss Cobbler

This delightful cobbler smells so good as it bakes that your mouth will be watering as you wait for it to finish cooking. Don't wait too long to try it: there will be no leftovers.
—**RONI GOODELL** SPANISH FORK, UT

PREP: 20 MIN. • **BAKE:** 25 MIN.
MAKES: 8 SERVINGS

½ cup packed brown sugar
3 tablespoons cornstarch
¼ teaspoon ground mace
¼ cup sherry or unsweetened
    apple juice
5 cups sliced peeled peaches
1 cup fresh or frozen blueberries
½ cup chopped pecans
1 tablespoon butter
1 tablespoon lemon juice
TOPPING
1 cup all-purpose flour
⅓ cup sugar
1½ teaspoons baking powder
    Dash salt
¼ cup cold butter, cubed
¼ cup milk
1 large egg, lightly beaten
    Whipped cream, optional

1. Preheat oven to 400°. In a large saucepan, combine brown sugar, cornstarch and mace. Stir in sherry until blended. Bring to a boil; cook and stir for 1-2 minutes or until thickened. Add peaches, blueberries, pecans, butter and lemon juice. Pour into a greased shallow 2-qt. baking dish.

2. For the topping, in a small bowl, combine flour, sugar, baking powder and salt. Cut in butter until coarse crumbs form. Stir in milk and egg. Spoon over the fruit mixture.

3. Bake for 25-30 minutes or until bubbly and a toothpick inserted in the topping comes out clean. Serve warm; if desired top with whipped cream.

NUTRITION FACTS 1 serving (calculated without whipped cream): 338 cal., 14g fat (5g sat. fat), 46mg chol., 162mg sod., 51g carb. (33g sugars, 3g fiber), 5g pro.

Gingersnap Rum Apple Crisp

My mother makes incredible apple crisp, and I've added a few twists of my own. We think it's best served warm with vanilla ice cream.

—NANCY HEISHMAN LAS VEGAS, NV

PREP: 25 MIN. • **BAKE:** 35 MIN.
MAKES: 8 SERVINGS

- ¾ cup packed brown sugar
- 3 tablespoons all-purpose flour
- 2¼ teaspoons ground cinnamon
- 1¼ teaspoons ground allspice
- 1 teaspoon salt
- ¼ teaspoon ground ginger
- 6 cups thinly sliced peeled tart apples (about 6 medium)
- 6 caramels
- ⅓ cup rum or orange juice

TOPPING
- ¾ cup crushed gingersnap cookies (about 15 cookies)
- ¾ cup packed brown sugar
- ½ cup all-purpose flour
- ½ cup cold butter, cubed
  Vanilla ice cream, optional

1. Preheat oven to 375°. In a large bowl, mix the first six ingredients. Add apples; toss to coat. In a small saucepan, combine caramels and rum. Cook and stir over medium-low heat until the caramels are melted. Pour over the apple mixture; toss to coat. Transfer to a greased 8-in.-square baking dish.

2. For the topping, in a small bowl, mix crushed cookies, brown sugar and flour; cut in butter until crumbly. Sprinkle over the filling. Bake 35-40 minutes or until the apples are tender. Cover loosely with foil if the top browns too quickly. Serve crisp warm, if desired with vanilla ice cream.

NUTRITION FACTS 1 serving (calculated without ice cream): 430 cal., 14g fat (8g sat. fat), 31mg chol., 483mg sod., 76g carb. (56g sugars, 2g fiber), 3g pro.

Blueberry Cornmeal Cobbler

I first came across this recipe many years ago. Cornbread, blueberries and maple syrup butter give this dessert a taste that's different from any cobbler you've had before.

—**JUDY WATSON** TIPTON, IN

PREP: 20 MIN. + STANDING • **BAKE:** 35 MIN.
MAKES: 12 SERVINGS

- 4   cups fresh blueberries
- 1   cup plus 2 tablespoons sugar
- 1   tablespoon quick-cooking tapioca
- 2   teaspoons grated lemon peel
- 1   teaspoon ground cinnamon
- ¼   to ½ teaspoon ground nutmeg

TOPPING

- ½   cup butter, softened, divided
- 1   cup confectioners' sugar
- 1   large egg
- 1   cup all-purpose flour
- ½   cup cornmeal
- 2   teaspoons baking powder
- ½   teaspoon baking soda
- ½   teaspoon salt
- ¾   cup buttermilk
- 2   tablespoons maple syrup

1. Preheat oven to 375°. In a large bowl, combine blueberries, sugar, tapioca, lemon peel, cinnamon and nutmeg. Let stand for 15 minutes. Pour into a greased 11x7-in. baking dish.

2. In a small bowl, beat ¼ cup of the butter and the confectioners' sugar. Add egg; beat well. Combine flour, cornmeal, baking powder, baking soda and salt; add to the creamed mixture alternately with buttermilk, beating just until combined. Pour over the berry mixture. Bake for 35-40 minutes or until a toothpick inserted in the center comes out clean.

3. In a small saucepan, melt remaining butter over low heat. Remove from the heat; stir in syrup. Brush over the corn bread. Broil 4-6 in. from heat for 1-2 minutes or until bubbly. Serve warm.

NUTRITION FACTS 1 serving: 290 cal., 9g fat (5g sat. fat), 39mg chol., 317mg sod., 52g carb. (35g sugars, 2g fiber), 3g pro.

Ginger-Lime Pear Cobbler

We have a huge pear tree in our yard, so I came up with a recipe to use the delicious fruit when it's in season. Tart lime, sweet pears and tangy ginger are a winning flavor combination in my book.

—**HEATHER NAAS** LOMPOC, CA

PREP: 25 MIN. • **BAKE:** 50 MIN. + COOLING
MAKES: 10 SERVINGS

- ¾ cup sugar
- ⅛ teaspoon ground ginger
- 5 cups sliced peeled fresh pears
- 2 tablespoons finely chopped crystallized ginger
- 2 tablespoons lime juice
- ½ cup butter, melted

BATTER
- ¾ cup all-purpose flour
- ½ cup sugar
- 2 teaspoons baking powder
- 1 teaspoon grated lime peel
- ⅛ teaspoon salt
  Pinch ground ginger
- ¾ cup whole milk

1. Preheat oven to 350°. In a large bowl, combine sugar and ground ginger. Stir in pears, crystallized ginger and lime juice; set aside.

2. Pour the butter into an ungreased 11x7-in. baking dish. In a small bowl, combine flour, sugar, baking powder, grated lime peel, salt and ginger. Stir in milk. Pour over the butter (do not stir). Spoon the pear mixture over the top.

3. Bake for 50-55 minutes or until bubbly and golden brown. Cool for 10 minutes before serving.

NUTRITION FACTS 1 serving: 281 cal., 10g fat (6g sat. fat), 26mg chol., 184mg sod., 49g carb. (35g sugars, 3g fiber), 2g pro.

DID YOU KNOW?

Among fruit desserts, cobblers are distinct—they use biscuits as the topping over a fruit filling. But crisps and crumbles can be confused for each other. In general, both have streusel toppings, but a crisp contains oats, while a crumble does not.

Plum Good Crisp

Packed with stone fruit and blueberries, this crisp goes well with any meal, but you can also serve it as a breakfast treat or a snack. When it's warm, it can't be beat.

—PETER HALFERTY CORPUS CHRISTI, TX

PREP: 20 MIN. • **BAKE:** 30 MIN. + STANDING
MAKES: 9 SERVINGS

---

4 cups sliced fresh plums (about 1½ pounds)
3 medium nectarines, sliced
1½ cups fresh blueberries
3 tablespoons brown sugar
2 tablespoons cornstarch
¼ cup maple syrup
2 tablespoons lemon juice
¼ teaspoon ground ginger
⅛ teaspoon ground nutmeg

TOPPING

½ cup all-purpose flour
½ cup old-fashioned oats
¼ cup packed brown sugar
¼ teaspoon salt
4 teaspoons unsweetened apple juice
4 teaspoons canola oil
1½ teaspoons butter, melted

1. In a large bowl, combine the plums, nectarines and blueberries. Combine the brown sugar, cornstarch, syrup, lemon juice, ginger and nutmeg until smooth; drizzle over plum mixture and toss to coat. Transfer to an 11x7-in. baking dish coated with cooking spray.

2. For topping, in a small bowl, combine the flour, oats, brown sugar and salt. Stir in the apple juice, oil and butter until crumbly. Sprinkle over fruit mixture.

3. Bake, uncovered, at 400° for 28-32 minutes or until bubbly and topping is golden brown. Let stand for 15 minutes. Serve warm.

NUTRITION FACTS 1 serving: 216 cal., 4g fat (1g sat. fat), 2mg chol., 78mg sod., 46g carb. (31g sugars, 3g fiber), 3g pro.

Walnut Pumpkin Cake Roll, p. 188

CHAPTER 8

CAKES & CUPCAKES

Layer cake, cupcakes, sheet cake, rolled cake—in all its variety, we love cake!

Banana Skillet Upside-Down Cake

My grandmother gave me my first cast-iron skillet, and I've been cooking and baking with it ever since. Sometimes I add drained maraschino cherries to this banana dessert and serve it with ice cream.

—TERRI MERRITTS NASHVILLE, TN

PREP: 25 MIN. • **BAKE:** 35 MIN.
MAKES: 10 SERVINGS

- 1 package (14 ounces) banana quick bread and muffin mix
- ½ cup chopped walnuts
- ¼ cup butter, cubed
- ¾ cup packed brown sugar
- 2 tablespoons lemon juice
- 4 medium bananas, cut into ¼-inch slices
- 2 cups flaked coconut

1. Preheat oven to 375°. Prepare banana bread batter according to the package directions; stir in walnuts.

2. In a 10-in. ovenproof skillet, melt butter over medium heat; stir in brown sugar until dissolved. Add the lemon juice; cook and stir 2-3 minutes longer or until slightly thickened. Remove from heat. Arrange bananas in a single layer over brown sugar mixture; sprinkle with the coconut.

3. Spoon prepared batter over coconut. Bake 35-40 minutes or until dark golden and a toothpick inserted in the center comes out clean. Cool for 5 minutes before inverting onto a serving plate. Serve warm.

NUTRITION FACTS 1 slice: 554 cal., 22g fat (10g sat. fat), 49mg chol., 459mg sod., 82g carb. (30g sugars, 2g fiber), 6g pro.

TOP TIP

If flaked coconut has been frozen or is dried out, make it fresh again by placing the desired amount in a bowl and sprinkling it with a few drops of water. Cover and microwave until warm.

SANDRA SOWARDS GAINESVILLE, FL

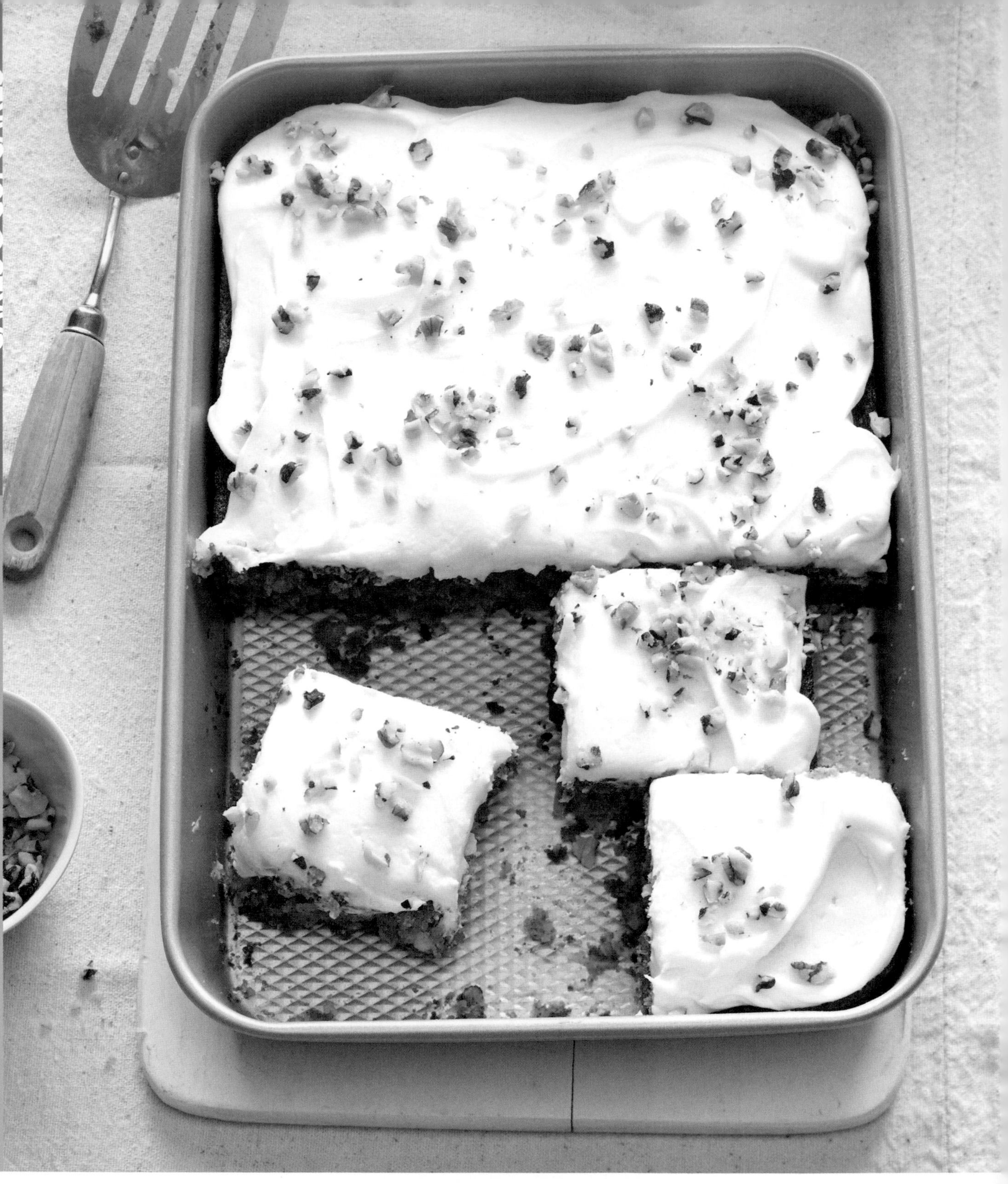

Carrot Cake

This wonderful recipe dates back to my great-grandmother. You'll love the moist texture the cake gets from pineapple, coconut and, of course, carrots! Traditional cream cheese frosting adds just the right touch of sweetness.

—DEBBIE TERENZINI-WILKERSON LUSBY, MD

PREP: 20 MIN. • **BAKE:** 50 MIN.
MAKES: 16 SERVINGS

- 2 cups all-purpose flour
- 2 cups sugar
- 2 teaspoons ground cinnamon
- 1 teaspoon baking soda
- ½ teaspoon salt
- 3 large eggs
- 1½ cups canola oil
- 2 cups finely grated carrots
- 1 teaspoon vanilla extract
- 1 cup well-drained crushed pineapple
- 1 cup flaked coconut
- 1 cup chopped nuts

CREAM CHEESE FROSTING
- 2 packages (3 ounces each) cream cheese, softened
- 6 tablespoons butter, softened
- 3 cups confectioners' sugar
- 1 teaspoon vanilla extract
  Additional chopped nuts

1. In a large bowl, combine the flour, sugar, cinnamon, baking soda and salt. Add the eggs, oil, carrots and vanilla; beat until combined. Stir in the pineapple, coconut and nuts.

2. Pour into a greased 13x9-in. baking pan. Bake at 350° for 50-60 minutes or until a toothpick inserted in the center comes out clean. Cool on a wire rack.

3. For frosting, beat cream cheese and butter in a small bowl until fluffy. Add the confectioners' sugar and vanilla; beat until smooth. Frost cake. Sprinkle with additional nuts. Store in the refrigerator.

NUTRITION FACTS 1 piece: 785 cal., 46g fat (12g sat. fat), 76mg chol., 326mg sod., 91g carb. (69g sugars, 2g fiber), 7g pro.

TOP TIP

Instead of peeling and grating carrots when making her special carrot cake, my grandma uses jars of baby food carrots (the third-stage carrots, designed for older babies, that have chunkier carrot puree).
—DIANE M. BAY CITY, MI

Amaretto Dream Cupcakes

Treat yourself to these indulgent little cupcakes laced with the irresistible flavor of amaretto and slivered almonds.

—ANETTE STEVENS OLDS, AB

PREP: 20 MIN. • **BAKE:** 15 MIN. + COOLING
MAKES: 2 DOZEN

¾ cup butter, softened
1½ cups packed brown sugar
2 large eggs
2 cups all-purpose flour
1½ teaspoons baking powder
½ teaspoon baking soda
¼ teaspoon salt
½ cup buttermilk
¼ cup amaretto
⅓ cup slivered almonds

AMARETTO BUTTER FROSTING

2 cups confectioners' sugar
¼ cup butter, melted
3 to 4 tablespoons heavy whipping cream
2 to 3 tablespoons amaretto

1. In a large bowl, cream butter and brown sugar until light and fluffy. Add eggs, one at a time, beating well after each.

2. Combine the flour, baking powder, baking soda and salt. Add to creamed mixture alternately with buttermilk and amaretto, beating well after each addition. Stir in almonds.

3. Fill 24 paper-lined muffins cups two-thirds full. Bake at 375° for 14-16 minutes or until a toothpick inserted in the center comes out clean. Cool for 5 minutes before removing from pans to wire racks to cool completely.

4. For the frosting, in a small bowl, beat the confectioners' sugar and butter. Add 3 tablespoons of the cream and 2 tablespoons of the amaretto; beat until smooth. Add remaining cream and amaretto if needed to achieve spreading consistency. Frost cupcakes.

NUTRITION FACTS 1 cupcake: 316 cal., 9g fat (5g sat. fat), 39mg chol., 180mg sod., 58g carb. (49g sugars, 0 fiber), 2g pro.

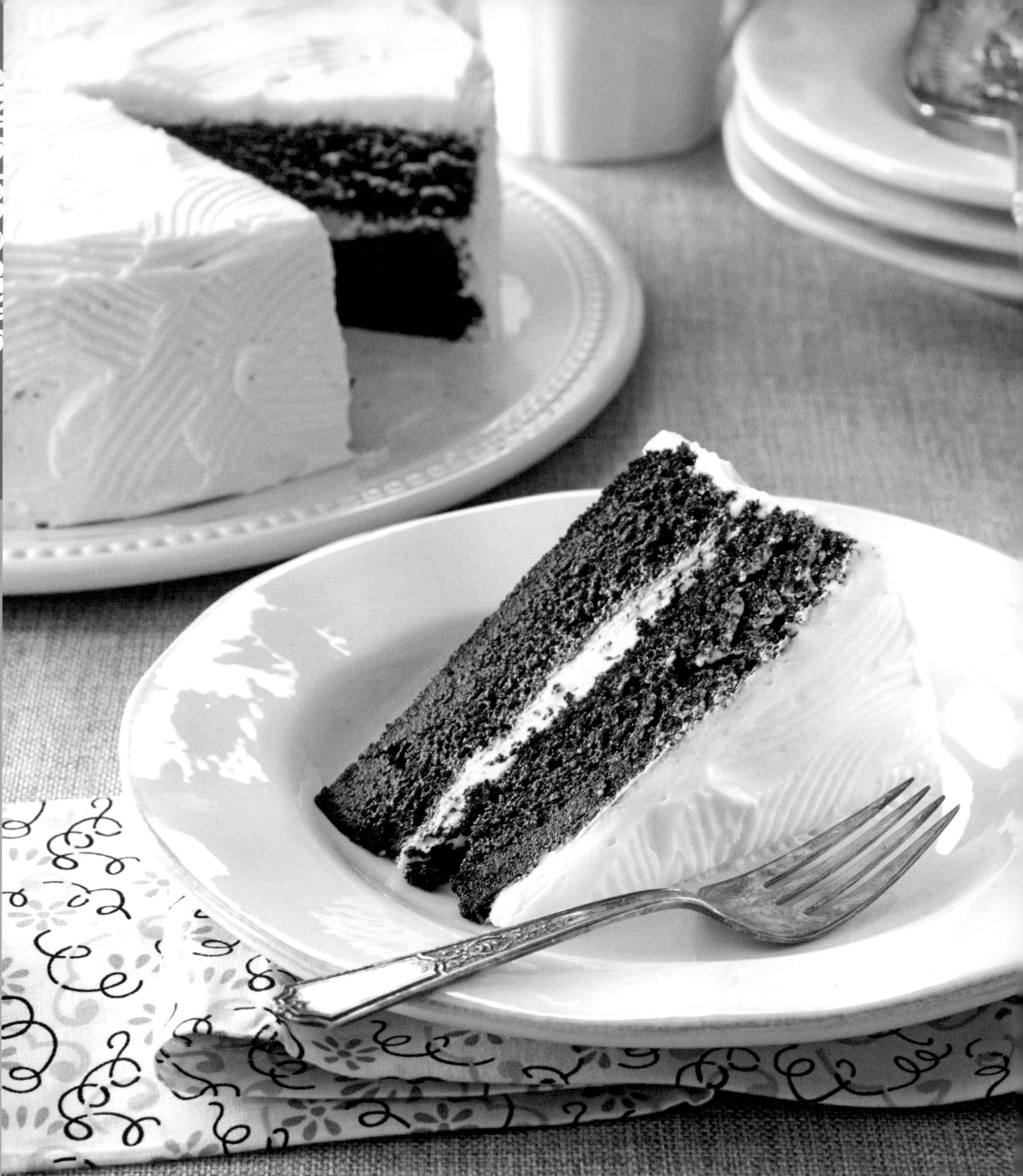

Moist Chocolate Cake

The cake reminds me of my grandmother, because it was one of her specialties. I bake it often for family parties, and it always brings fond memories. The cake is light and lovely with a delicious chocolate taste.

—PATRICIA KREITZ RICHLAND, PA

PREP: 15 MIN. • **BAKE:** 25 MIN. + COOLING
MAKES: 12 SERVINGS

- 2 cups all-purpose flour
- 1 teaspoon salt
- 1 teaspoon baking powder
- 2 teaspoons baking soda
- ¾ cup baking cocoa
- 2 cups sugar
- 1 cup canola oil
- 1 cup brewed coffee
- 1 cup milk
- 2 large eggs
- 1 teaspoon vanilla extract

FAVORITE ICING
- 1 cup milk
- 5 tablespoons all-purpose flour
- ½ cup butter, softened
- ½ cup shortening
- 1 cup sugar
- 1 teaspoon vanilla extract

1. Preheat oven to 325°. Sift together ingredients in a bowl. Add oil, coffee and milk; mix at medium speed 1 minute. Add eggs and vanilla; beat 2 minutes longer. (Batter will be thin.)

2. Pour into two greased and floured 9-in. round baking pans (or two 8-in. round baking pans and six muffin cups).

3. Bake until a toothpick inserted in the center comes out clean, 25-30 minutes. Cool 10 minutes before removing from pans. Cool on wire racks.

4. Meanwhile, for icing, combine milk and flour in a saucepan; cook until thick. Cover and refrigerate.

5. In a bowl, beat butter, shortening, sugar and vanilla until creamy. Add the chilled milk mixture and beat for 10 minutes. Frost cooled cake.

NUTRITION FACTS 1 slice: 636 cal., 37g fat (10g sat. fat), 61mg chol., 549mg sod., 73g carb. (51g sugars, 2g fiber), 6g pro.

Pumpkin Cake Roll

...my family's favorite dessert
...lly for holiday gatherings.
CENTER RUTLAND, VT

PREP: 20 MIN. + CHILLING
BAKE: 15 MIN. + COOLING
MAKES: 12 SERVINGS

3	large eggs
1	cup sugar
⅔	cup canned pumpkin
1	teaspoon lemon juice
¾	cup all-purpose flour
2	teaspoons ground cinnamon
1	teaspoon baking powder
1	teaspoon ground ginger
½	teaspoon salt
½	teaspoon ground nutmeg
1	cup finely chopped walnuts
	Confectioners' sugar

FILLING

6	ounces cream cheese, softened
1	cup confectioners' sugar
¼	cup butter, softened
½	teaspoon vanilla extract

1. Line a greased 15x10x 1-in. baking pan with waxed paper. Grease the paper; set aside. In a bowl, beat eggs for 3 minutes. Gradually add sugar; beat for 2 minutes or until mixture becomes thick and lemon-colored. Stir in pumpkin and lemon juice. Combine dry ingredients; fold into the pumpkin mixture. Spread batter evenly in prepared pan. Sprinkle with walnuts.

2. Bake at 375° for 12-14 minutes or until cake springs back when lightly touched in center. Cool for 5 minutes. Turn cake out of pan onto a kitchen towel dusted with confectioners' sugar. Gently peel off waxed paper. Roll up cake in towel jelly-roll style, starting with a long side. Cool completely on a wire rack.

3. In a bowl, combine filling ingredients; beat until smooth. Unroll cake; spread evenly with the filling to within ½ in. of edges. Roll up again, without towel. Cover and refrigerate for 1 hour before cutting. Refrigerate leftovers.

NUTRITION FACTS 1 slice: 312 cal., 17g fat (7g sat. fat), 81mg chol., 247mg sod., 36g carb. (26g sugars, 2g fiber), 6g pro.

CAKES & CUPCAKES

Boston Cream Cupcakes

Boston cream bismarcks have been my favorite bakery treat since I was a child, so I put together this easy-to-make cupcake version.

—**JEANNE HOLT** MENDOTA HEIGHTS, MN

PREP: 25 MIN. • **BAKE:** 15 MIN. + COOLING
MAKES: ½ DOZEN

3 tablespoons shortening
⅓ cup sugar
1 large egg
½ teaspoon vanilla extract
½ cup all-purpose flour
½ teaspoon baking powder
¼ teaspoon salt
3 tablespoons 2% milk
⅔ cup prepared vanilla pudding
½ cup semisweet chocolate chips
¼ cup heavy whipping cream

1. In a small bowl, cream shortening and sugar until light and fluffy. Beat in egg. Beat in vanilla. Combine the flour, baking powder and salt; add to the creamed mixture alternately with milk, beating well after each addition.

2. Fill paper-lined muffin cups half full. Bake at 350° for 15-20 minutes or until a toothpick inserted in the center comes out clean. Cool for 10 minutes before removing from pan to a wire rack to cool completely.

3. Cut a small hole in the corner of a pastry or plastic bag; insert a small tip. Fill with pudding. Push the tip through the top to fill each cupcake.

4. Place chocolate chips in a small bowl. In a small saucepan, bring cream just to a boil. Pour over chocolate; whisk until smooth. Cool, stirring occasionally, to room temperature or until ganache thickens slightly, about 10 minutes. Spoon over cupcakes. Let stand until set. Store in an airtight container in the refrigerator.

NUTRITION FACTS 1 cupcake: 288 cal., 16g fat (7g sat. fat), 53mg chol., 198mg sod., 35g carb. (22g sugars, 1g fiber), 4g pro.

Moist Lemon Chiffon Cake

This fluffy, airy cake is a real treat drizzled with its sweet-tart lemon glaze.

—REBECCA BAIRD SALT LAKE CITY, UTAH

PREP: 15 MIN.
BAKE: 45 MIN. + COOLING
MAKES: 16 SERVINGS

½ cup fat-free evaporated milk
½ cup reduced-fat sour cream
¼ cup lemon juice
2 tablespoons canola oil
2 teaspoons vanilla extract
1 teaspoon grated lemon peel
1 teaspoon lemon extract
2 cups cake flour
1½ cups sugar
1 tablespoon baking powder
½ teaspoon salt
1 cup large egg whites (about 7)
½ teaspoon cream of tartar

LEMON GLAZE

1¾ cups confectioners' sugar
3 tablespoons lemon juice

1. Preheat oven to 325°. In a large bowl, combine the first seven ingredients. Sift together the flour, sugar, baking powder and salt; gradually beat into the lemon mixture until smooth. In a small bowl, beat egg whites until foamy. Add cream of tartar; beat until stiff peaks form. Gently fold into the lemon mixture.

2. Pour batter into an ungreased 10-in. tube pan. Bake for 45-55 minutes or until cake springs back when lightly touched. Immediately invert the pan; cool completely. Remove the cake to a serving platter. Combine the glaze ingredients; drizzle over the cake.

NUTRITION FACTS 1 slice: 230 cal., 3g fat (1g sat. fat), 3mg chol., 189mg sod., 47g carb. (33g sugars, 0 fiber), 4g pro.

Milk Cake

This is a simple recipe—and especially easy in a well-seasoned cast-iron skillet. The result is a deliciously light, airy cake.
—**SUZANNE COLEMAN** RABUN GAP, GA

PREP: 20 MIN. • **BAKE:** 30 MIN.
MAKES: 8 SERVINGS

½   cup milk
¾   cup all-purpose flour
1   teaspoon baking powder
¼   teaspoon salt
3   large eggs, room temperature
1   teaspoon vanilla extract
1   cup sugar
TOPPING
⅓   cup packed brown sugar
½   cup chopped pecans
2   tablespoons butter, softened
2   tablespoons milk
1   cup flaked coconut

1. Scald milk; set aside. Combine flour, baking powder and salt; set aside. In a bowl, beat eggs until thick and lemon-colored; stir in vanilla. Gradually add sugar, blending well. On low speed, alternately mix in milk and the dry ingredients. Pour batter into a greased 10-in. cast-iron skillet.

2. Bake at 350° for 25-30 minutes or until the cake springs back when lightly touched. Remove cake and preheat broiler. Combine all topping ingredients and sprinkle over cake. Broil 5 in. from the heat until topping bubbles and turns golden brown. Serve warm.

NUTRITION FACTS 1 slice: 349 cal., 15g fat (7g sat. fat), 90mg chol., 220mg sod., 51g carb. (39g sugars, 2g fiber), 5g pro.

DID YOU KNOW?

Don't use dish soap on a cast-iron skillet; it will remove the seasoning. Instead, rinse it with hot water, using a stiff nylon brush or coarse-grained sea salt or kosher salt to remove residue. Towel-dry and apply a light coat of oil while the pan is warm.

Cherry Cheese Cupcakes

Our church Christmas party always includes these pretty cupcakes as my home-baked contribution. I add mint leaves for a cheery holiday garnish.

—**LEANNE BEAGLEY** ROCHESTER, NY

PREP: 20 MIN. • **BAKE:** 35 MIN. + COOLING
MAKES: ABOUT 2 DOZEN

    3   packages (8 ounces each) cream
        cheese, softened
1½ cups sugar, divided
1½ teaspoons vanilla extract, divided
    5   large eggs
    1   cup sour cream
1½ cups cherry pie filling
        Mint leaves, optional

1. In a large bowl, beat cream cheese, 1 cup sugar and 1 teaspoon vanilla until smooth. Add eggs, one at a time, beating well after each addition.

2. Spoon into foil-lined muffin cups. Bake at 300° for 25-30 minutes or until a toothpick inserted in the center comes out clean. Cool for 5 minutes.

3. In a small bowl, combine sour cream and the remaining sugar and vanilla until smooth. Spoon onto cupcakes. Return to the oven for 6-8 minutes or until set. Cool for 10 minutes before removing from pans to wire racks. Cool completely.

4. Top with pie filling; garnish with mint if desired. Store in the refrigerator.

NUTRITION FACTS 1 cupcake: 202 cal., 13g fat (8g sat. fat), 82mg chol., 105mg sod., 18g carb. (17g sugars, 0 fiber), 4g pro.

Spiced Devil's Food Cake

One of my mom's friends gave her this recipe when I was a child and it has been a family favorite ever since. When your chocolate sweet tooth acts up, this really hits the spot!

—LINDA YEAMANS ASHLAND, OR

PREP: 25 MIN. • **BAKE:** 30 MIN. + COOLING
MAKES: 12 SERVINGS

---

1   cup butter, softened
1½ cups granulated sugar
3   large eggs
1   teaspoon vanilla extract
2   cups all-purpose flour
¼   cup baking cocoa
1   teaspoon baking powder
1   teaspoon baking soda
1   teaspoon ground cinnamon
½   to 1 teaspoon ground nutmeg
¼   to ½ teaspoon ground cloves
1   cup buttermilk

MOCHA ICING
3¾ cups confectioners' sugar
¼   cup baking cocoa
6   tablespoons strong brewed coffee
6   tablespoons butter, melted
1   teaspoon vanilla extract
     Toasted whole or chopped almonds, optional

1. Preheat oven to 350°. Cream butter and granulated sugar until light and fluffy. Add eggs, one at a time, beating well after each addition. Add vanilla.

2. Sift together all dry ingredients; add to creamed mixture alternately with buttermilk. Pour into two greased and floured 9-in. round baking pans.

3. Bake until a toothpick inserted in center comes out clean, 30-35 minutes. Cool on wire racks for 10 minutes before removing from pans.

4. In a small bowl, combine all icing ingredients except nuts. Spread frosting between the layers and over the top and sides of cake. If desired, top with toasted almonds.

NUTRITION FACTS 1 slice: 543 cal., 23g fat (14g sat. fat), 110mg chol., 389mg sod., 82g carb. (61g sugars, 1g fiber), 5g pro.

Chocolate Macaroon Cupcakes

A delightful coconut and ricotta cheese filling is hidden inside these cupcakes.
—**DOLORES SKROUT** SUMMERHILL, PA

PREP: 20 MIN. • **BAKE:** 30 MIN. + COOLING
MAKES: 1½ DOZEN

2   large egg whites
1   large egg
⅓   cup unsweetened applesauce
1   teaspoon vanilla extract
1¼ cups all-purpose flour
1   cup sugar
⅓   cup baking cocoa
½   teaspoon baking soda
¾   cup buttermilk

FILLING
1   cup reduced-fat ricotta cheese
¼   cup sugar
1   large egg white
⅓   cup flaked coconut
½   teaspoon coconut or almond
    extract
2   teaspoons confectioners' sugar

1. In a bowl, combine the egg whites, egg, applesauce and vanilla. Combine the flour, sugar, cocoa and baking soda; gradually add to the egg white mixture alternately with buttermilk. Spoon half of the batter into 18 muffin cups coated with cooking spray.

2. In another bowl, beat the ricotta cheese, sugar and egg white until smooth. Stir in coconut and extract. Spoon 1 tablespoonful in the center of each muffin cup.

3. Fill muffin cups two-thirds full with remaining batter. Bake at 350° for 28-33 minutes or until a toothpick inserted in cupcake comes out clean. Cool for 5 minutes before removing from pans to wire racks; cool completely. Dust with confectioners' sugar.

NUTRITION FACTS 1 cupcake: 125 cal., 1g fat (1g sat. fat), 13mg chol., 87mg sod., 25g carb. (16g sugars, 1g fiber), 4g pro. *Diabetic Exchanges:* 1½ starch.

Aunt Lou's Fresh Apple Cake

My Great-Aunt Lou made a richly fragrant apple cake that became a family tradition. My mom makes it for our annual beach trip to the Outer Banks.

—**CRISTY KING** SCOTT DEPOT, WV

PREP: 15 MIN. • **BAKE:** 50 MIN. + COOLING
MAKES: 12 SERVINGS

- 2 cups sugar
- 1 cup canola oil
- 3 large eggs
- 2 teaspoons vanilla extract
- 3 cups all-purpose flour
- 1 teaspoon salt
- 1 teaspoon baking powder
- 3 cups chopped peeled apples (about 3 medium)
  Confectioners' sugar

1. Preheat oven to 350°. Grease and flour a 10-in. fluted tube pan.

2. In a large bowl, beat the sugar, oil, eggs and vanilla until well blended. In another bowl, whisk flour, salt and baking powder; gradually beat into oil mixture. Stir in apples. Transfer batter to prepared pan.

3. Bake for 50-60 minutes or until a toothpick inserted in center comes out clean. Cool in pan for 10 minutes. Run a knife around sides and center tube of the pan. Remove cake to a wire rack and allow to cool completely. Dust with confectioners' sugar.

NOTE To remove cakes easily, use solid shortening to grease plain and fluted tube pans.

NUTRITION FACTS 1 slice: 445 cal., 20g fat (2g sat. fat), 47mg chol., 249mg sod., 62g carb. (37g sugars, 2g fiber), 5g pro.

HOW TO

DUST WITH CONFECTIONERS' SUGAR
Place confectioners' sugar in a small metal sieve or sifter; shake or sift over the top of the baked and cooled cake. To make a pattern, lay a doily over the cake; sift an even layer of sugar over all. Lift the doily straight up, leaving the pattern on the cake.

**Lovely Lemon
Cheesecake, p. 214**

CHAPTER 9

CHEESECAKES

Try these exciting twists on the ultimate in decadent desserts.

CHEESECAKES

Caramel Pecan Cheesecake

I created this creamy cheesecake using two favorites—caramel and pecans. It's a stunning cake that rivals any I've tasted.

—DEIDRE SIZER CEDARVILLE, OH

PREP: 30 MIN.
BAKE: 1¼ HOURS + CHILLING
MAKES: 12 SERVINGS

- 2 cups crushed shortbread cookies
- 3 tablespoons butter, melted
- ¼ cup plus 2 tablespoons all-purpose flour, divided
- 1 jar (12¼ ounces) caramel ice cream topping
- 1 cup chopped pecans
- 5 packages (8 ounces each) cream cheese, softened
- 1¾ cups sugar
- 1½ teaspoons vanilla extract
- 4 large eggs
- 2 large egg yolks
- ⅓ cup heavy whipping cream

SOUR CREAM TOPPING

- 2 cups sour cream
- ⅓ cup sugar

1. Preheat oven to 350°. In a small bowl, combine cookie crumbs and butter. Press into the bottom and 1 in. up the sides of a greased 10-in. springform pan. Place the pan on a baking sheet. Bake 8-10 minutes or until set. Cool on a wire rack.

2. Set oven to 325°. In a small bowl, stir ¼ cup of flour into the caramel topping. Set aside ⅓ cup of the caramel mixture and 2 tablespoons of pecans. Drizzle the remaining caramel mixture over the crust; sprinkle with remaining pecans.

3. In a large bowl, beat cream cheese, sugar, vanilla and the remaining flour until smooth. Beat in eggs and yolks just until combined. Stir in cream.

4. Pour the batter over the crust. Bake for 65-70 minutes or until the center is almost set.

5. In a small bowl, combine sour cream and sugar; carefully spread over the warm filling. Bake 10-12 minutes longer or until topping is set. Cool on a wire rack for 10 minutes. Run a knife around edge of pan to loosen; cool 1 hour longer.

6. Chill for 8 hours or overnight. Remove the sides of the pan. Just before serving, drizzle cake with the reserved caramel mixture and sprinkle with the reserved pecans. Refrigerate any leftovers.

NUTRITION FACTS 1 slice: 858 cal., 58g fat (31g sat. fat), 255mg chol., 510mg sod., 72g carb. (37g sugars, 2g fiber), 14g pro.

Easy Mini Caramel Apple Cheesecakes

Cheesecake is the ultimate comfort food, but a big slice can be too rich. These muffin-sized cheesecakes topped with apples and creamy caramel dazzle the senses without overwhelming them.

—BRANDIE CRANSHAW RAPID CITY, SD

PREP: 30 MIN. • **BAKE:** 15 MIN. + COOLING
MAKES: 1 DOZEN

1   cup graham cracker crumbs
2   tablespoons sugar
¼   teaspoon ground cinnamon
3   tablespoons butter, melted
CHEESECAKE
2   packages (8 ounces each) cream cheese, softened
½   cup sugar
1   teaspoon vanilla extract
2   large eggs, lightly beaten
TOPPING
1   large apple, peeled and finely chopped
1   tablespoon butter
1   tablespoon sugar
¼   teaspoon ground cinnamon
     Dash ground cloves
½   cup butterscotch-caramel ice cream topping

1. Preheat oven to 350°. Line 12 muffin cups with paper liners.

2. In a small bowl, mix cracker crumbs, sugar and cinnamon; stir in melted butter. Spoon 1 rounded tablespoon crumb mixture into each muffin cup; press down with a narrow glass or spoon.

3. In a large bowl, beat cream cheese and sugar until smooth. Beat in vanilla. Add eggs; beat on low speed just until blended. Pour over crusts.

4. Bake 15-18 minutes or until centers are set (do not overbake). Cool in pan on a wire rack 30 minutes.

5. To serve, in a small skillet, cook and stir chopped apple with butter, sugar, cinnamon and cloves over medium heat 4-5 minutes or until tender; stir in caramel topping. Spoon over the cheesecakes. Refrigerate leftovers.

NUTRITION FACTS 1 cheesecake with about 1 tablespoon topping: 307 cal., 19g fat (10g sat. fat), 84mg chol., 244mg sod., 31g carb. (23g sugars, 0 fiber), 4g pro.

Cranberry Mocha Cheesecake

I've made this festive dessert for quite a few occasions; cranberries make it a perfect finale to a holiday dinner.

—**ANISSA BEDNARSKI** ORONOCO, MN

PREP: 30 MIN. + COOLING
BAKE: 50 MIN. + CHILLING
MAKES: 14 SERVINGS

- 1 package (9 ounces) chocolate wafer cookies, crushed
- 1/3 cup butter, melted

FILLING

- 4 packages (8 ounces each) cream cheese, softened
- 1 1/3 cups sugar
- 1 tablespoon all-purpose flour
- 4 large eggs
- 2 tablespoons instant coffee granules
- 1 tablespoon hot water
- 1/4 cup heavy whipping cream
- 1 1/2 teaspoons ground cinnamon

TOPPING

- 1 tablespoon cornstarch
- 1 can (14 ounces) whole-berry cranberry sauce
- 3/4 cup heavy whipping cream
- 1/2 teaspoon vanilla extract
- 2 tablespoons confectioners' sugar

1. Preheat oven to 350°. Combine cookie crumbs and butter; press into the bottom and 2 in. up the sides of a greased 9-in. springform pan; set aside. In a large bowl, beat cream cheese until smooth. Combine sugar and flour; add to cream cheese and mix well. Add the eggs; beat on low just until combined.

2. In a small bowl, dissolve coffee in water; add cream and cinnamon. Stir into the cream cheese mixture just until blended. Pour over the crust. Place pan on a baking sheet.

3. Bake 50-55 minutes or until center is almost set. Cool on a wire rack for 10 minutes. Run a knife around the edge of the pan to loosen; cool 1 hour longer.

4. In a large saucepan, bring cornstarch and cranberry sauce to a boil. Cook and stir for 2 minutes or until thickened. Cool.

5. In a small bowl, beat cream and vanilla until soft peaks form. Gradually add confectioners' sugar, beating until stiff peaks form. Spread over the cheesecake. Refrigerate for 20 minutes or until set.

6. Spread 1 cup of the cranberry mixture to within 1 in. of edge. Refrigerate the cheesecake and the remaining cranberry mixture overnight. Serve cake with the remaining cranberry mixture.

NUTRITION FACTS 1 piece: 384 cal., 20g fat (11g sat. fat), 114mg chol., 230mg sod., 48g carb. (28g sugars, 1g fiber), 5g pro.

Old-World Ricotta Cheesecake

I reconstructed this dessert based on an old recipe that had been in the family for years but had never been written down. The cinnamon flavor of the zwieback crust and the dense texture of the ricotta remind me of the cheesecake I enjoyed as a child.

—**MARY BETH JUNG** HENDERSONVILLE, NC

PREP: 20 MIN. • **BAKE:** 1 HOUR + CHILLING
MAKES: 12 SERVINGS

1⅔ cups zwieback crumbs
3 tablespoons sugar
½ teaspoon ground cinnamon
⅓ cup butter, softened

FILLING
2 cartons (15 ounces each) ricotta cheese
½ cup sugar
½ cup half-and-half cream
2 tablespoons all-purpose flour
1 tablespoon lemon juice
1 teaspoon finely grated lemon peel
¼ teaspoon salt
2 large eggs, lightly beaten

TOPPING
1 cup sour cream
2 tablespoons sugar
1 teaspoon vanilla extract

1. Combine zwieback crumbs, sugar and cinnamon; mix in butter until mixture is crumbled. Press mixture into the bottom and 1½ in. up the sides of a greased 9-in. springform pan. Refrigerate until chilled.

2. Preheat oven to 350°. Combine all filling ingredients except eggs and beat until smooth. Add eggs; beat on low until combined. Pour into crust. Place pan on a baking sheet.

3. Bake until center is set, about 50 minutes. Remove from oven; let stand 15 minutes, leaving oven on. Combine the topping ingredients; spoon around the edge of the cheesecake. Carefully spread the topping over the filling. Bake 10 minutes longer. Use a knife to loosen the sides of the cake from the pan; cool for 1 hour. Refrigerate cake 3 hours or overnight, covering when completely cooled. To serve, remove rim from pan. Refrigerate leftovers.

NUTRITION FACTS 1 slice: 260 cal., 14g fat (9g sat. fat), 83mg chol., 191mg sod., 25g carb. (16g sugars, 0 fiber), 7g pro.

Lovely Lemon Cheesecake

Just wait for the "oohs!" and "aahs!" when you present this luxurious cheesecake. The lemon flavor gives it a bright and tangy flair.

—MARGARET ALLEN ABINGDON, VA

PREP: 25 MIN. • **BAKE:** 70 MIN. + CHILLING
MAKES: 14 SERVINGS

- ¾ cup graham cracker crumbs
- 2 tablespoons sugar
- 3 teaspoons ground cinnamon
- 2 tablespoons butter, melted

FILLING

- 5 packages (8 ounces each) cream cheese, softened
- 1⅔ cups sugar
- ⅛ teaspoon salt
- ¼ cup lemon juice
- 1½ teaspoons vanilla extract
- 5 large eggs, lightly beaten
  Thin lemon slices, optional

1. Preheat oven to 325°. Place a greased 10-in. springform pan on a double thickness of heavy-duty foil (about 18 in. square). Wrap foil securely around pan.

2. In a small bowl, mix cracker crumbs, sugar and cinnamon; stir in butter. Press mixture into the bottom of the prepared pan; refrigerate.

3. In a large bowl, beat cream cheese, sugar and salt until smooth. Beat in lemon juice and vanilla. Add eggs; beat on low speed just until blended. Pour over crust. Place the springform pan in a larger baking pan; add 1 in. of hot water to the larger pan.

4. Bake for 70-80 minutes or until the center is just set and the top appears dull. Remove springform pan from water bath. Cool cheesecake on a wire rack for 10 minutes. Loosen sides from pan with a knife; remove foil. Cool 1 hour longer. Refrigerate overnight, covering when completely cooled.

5. Remove rim from pan. If desired, top cheesecake with lemon slices.

NUTRITION FACTS 1 slice (calculated without lemon slices): 444 cal., 32g fat (19g sat. fat), 169mg chol., 325mg sod., 32g carb. (27g sugars, 0 fiber), 9g pro.

DID YOU KNOW?

Cutting cheesecake can be a "drag"— literally. To cut slices of cheesecake without the dragged edges, use a straight-edge knife. Warm the blade in hot water, dry it and then slice. Clean and rewarm the knife after each cut.

Pumpkin Cheesecake

When I was young we produced several ingredients for this longtime favorite on the farm. We raised pumpkins in our large vegetable garden, and made homemade butter and lots of sour cream from our dairy herd.

—EVONNE WURMNEST NORMAL, IL

PREP: 20 MIN. + CHILLING
BAKE: 55 MIN. + COOLING
MAKES: 12-16 SERVINGS

CRUST

- 1   cup graham cracker crumbs
- 1   tablespoon sugar
- ¼   cup butter, melted

FILLING

- 2   packages (8 ounces each) cream cheese, softened
- ¾   cup sugar
- 2   large eggs
- 1   can (15 ounces) solid-pack pumpkin
- 1¼ teaspoons ground cinnamon
- ½   teaspoon ground ginger
- ½   teaspoon ground nutmeg
- ¼   teaspoon salt

TOPPING

- 2   cups (16 ounces) sour cream
- 2   tablespoons sugar
- 1   teaspoon vanilla extract
- 12 to 16 pecan halves, chopped

1. In a small bowl, combine graham cracker crumbs and sugar; stir in butter. Press into the bottom of a 9-in. springform pan; chill.

2. For filling, in a large bowl, beat cream cheese and sugar until smooth. Add eggs, beat on low speed just until combined. Stir in pumpkin, spices and salt.

3. Pour filling into the crust. Place pan on a baking sheet. Bake at 350° for 50 minutes.

4. For topping, combine sour cream, sugar and vanilla until smooth. Spread over filling; return to the oven for 5 minutes. Cool on rack for 10 minutes. Carefully run a knife around the edge of the pan to loosen; cool 1 hour longer.

5. Refrigerate overnight. Remove the sides of the pan. Top with chopped pecans. Refrigerate leftovers.

NUTRITION FACTS 1 slice: 230 calories, 15g fat (9g sat. fat), 70mg chol., 164mg sod., 20g carb. (15g sugars, 2g fiber), 4g pro.

Maple-Nut Cheesecake

To vary this versatile cheesecake, add cherries to the top or swirl raspberry jam throughout before baking it.

—**WENDY PAFFENROTH** PINE ISLAND, NY

PREP: 45 MIN. • **BAKE:** 45 MIN. + CHILLING
MAKES: 12 SERVINGS

¾ cup graham cracker crumbs
½ cup finely chopped walnuts
3 tablespoons sugar
¼ cup butter, melted

FILLING

4 packages (8 ounces each) cream
   cheese, softened
¾ cup sugar
2 teaspoons maple flavoring
½ teaspoon almond extract
⅛ teaspoon grated lemon peel
3 large eggs, lightly beaten
   Melted chocolate, optional

1. Preheat oven to 325°. Place a greased 9-in. springform pan on a double thickness of heavy-duty foil (about 18 in. square). Wrap foil securely around pan.

2. In a small bowl, mix the cracker crumbs, walnuts and sugar; stir in butter. Press into the bottom and 1 in. up the sides of the prepared pan. Place the pan on a baking sheet. Bake crust 10 minutes. Cool on a wire rack.

3. For filling, in a large bowl, beat cream cheese and sugar until smooth. Beat in maple flavoring, extract and lemon peel. Add eggs; beat on low speed just until blended. Pour into the crust. Place the springform pan in a larger baking pan; add 1 in. of hot water to the larger pan.

4. Bake for 45-55 minutes or until the center is just set and top appears dull. Remove springform pan from water bath. Cool cheesecake on a wire rack for 10 minutes. Loosen sides from pan with a knife; remove foil. Cool 1 hour longer. Refrigerate overnight.

5. Remove rim from pan. If desired, drizzle the cooled cheesecake with melted chocolate.

NUTRITION FACTS 1 slice: 434 cal., 35g fat (20g sat. fat), 146mg chol., 300mg sod., 22g carb. (18g sugars, 0 fiber), 8g pro.

TOP TIP

Why bake cheesecake in a hot water bath? You can often do without, but the hot water makes a milder kind of heat than direct oven heat, and it adds moisture. As a result, a cheesecake cooked that way stays tender and is less likely to crack.

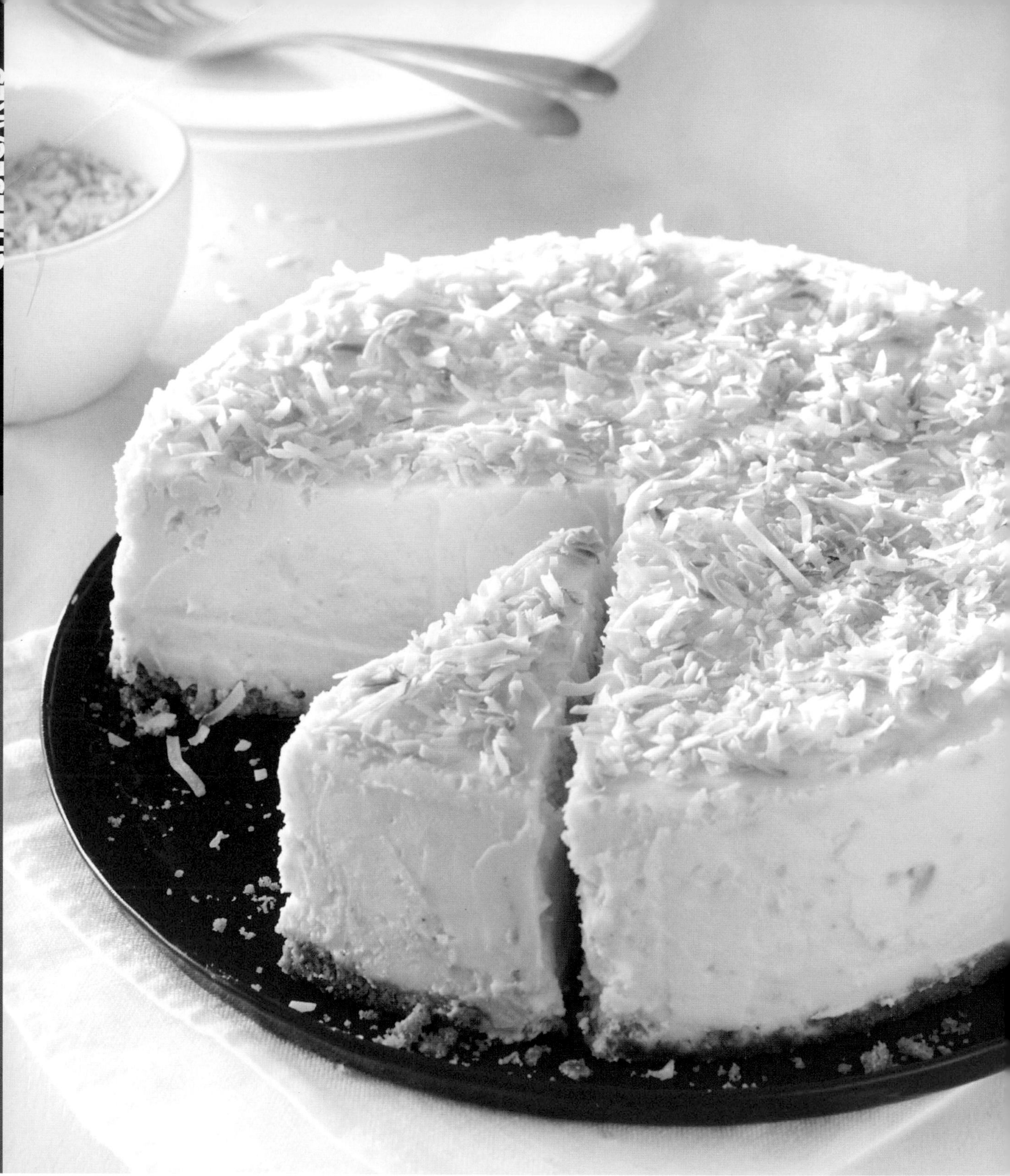

Coconut-White Chocolate Cheesecake

Friends repeatedly suggested that I submit this creation for publication—and so I finally did! For the best texture, make sure not to overmix the batter.

—**JAMIE HARRIS** DANVILLE, IL

PREP: 40 MIN. • **BAKE:** 1 HOUR + CHILLING
MAKES: 16 SERVINGS

1½ cups graham cracker crumbs
6 tablespoons butter, melted
5 packages (8 ounces each) cream cheese, softened
1 cup sugar
1½ cups white baking chips, melted and cooled
¾ cup coconut milk
2 teaspoons coconut extract
1 teaspoon vanilla extract
4 large eggs, lightly beaten
¾ cup flaked coconut, toasted, divided

1. Preheat oven to 325°. Place a greased 9x3-in. springform pan on a double thickness of heavy-duty foil (about 18 in. square). Wrap the foil securely around the pan.

2. In a small bowl, mix cracker crumbs and butter. Press the crumb mixture into the bottom of the prepared pan.

3. In a large bowl, beat cream cheese and sugar until smooth. Beat in cooled chips, coconut milk and extracts. Add eggs; beat on low just until blended. Fold in ½ cup of the coconut. Pour over crust. Place the springform pan in a larger baking pan; add 1 in. of hot water to the larger pan.

4. Bake 60-70 minutes or until the center is just set and the top appears dull. Remove springform pan from the water bath. Cool cheesecake on a wire rack for 10 minutes. Loosen the sides from pan with a knife; remove the foil. Cool 1 hour longer. Refrigerate overnight, covering when completely cooled.

5. Remove the rim from pan. Serve cheesecake topped with the remaining toasted coconut.

NOTE To toast coconut, bake in a shallow pan in a 350° oven for 5-10 minutes or cook in a skillet over low heat until golden brown, stirring occasionally.

NUTRITION FACTS 1 slice: 517 cal., 40g fat (25g sat. fat), 144mg chol., 332mg sod., 32g carb. (26g sugars, 1g fiber), 9g pro.

Pistachio Cardamom Cheesecake

Cardamom's sweet, warm taste makes me think of cloves, allspice and pepper all at once. This spice plus pistachios transforms cheesecake into an exotic dessert.

—**CAROLYN HARKONNEN** LOOMIS, CA

PREP: 30 MIN. • **BAKE:** 35 MIN. + CHILLING
MAKES: 12 SERVINGS

1¼ cups finely crushed animal crackers
3 tablespoons packed brown sugar
¼ cup butter, melted

FILLING
2 packages (8 ounces each) cream cheese, softened
1 can (14 ounces) sweetened condensed milk
1 tablespoon lemon juice
1½ teaspoons ground cardamom
1 drop green food coloring (optional)
3 large eggs, lightly beaten
½ cup pistachios, finely chopped
Sweetened whipped cream, optional
Additional chopped pistachios and animal cracker crumbs (optional)

1. Preheat oven to 325°. Place a greased 9-in. springform pan on a double thickness of heavy-duty foil (about 18 in. square). Securely wrap foil around pan.

2. In a small bowl, combine the cracker crumbs and brown sugar; stir in butter. Press onto the bottom of prepared pan. Place pan on a baking sheet. Bake for 15 minutes. Cool on a wire rack.

3. Beat cream cheese until smooth. Beat in milk, lemon juice, cardamom and, if desired, food coloring. Add eggs; beat on low just until combined. Fold in the pistachios. Pour over crust. Place pan in a large baking pan; add 1 in. of boiling water to larger pan.

4. Bake for 35-40 minutes or until center is just set and top appears dull. Remove pan from water bath; remove foil. Cool on a wire rack for 10 minutes; loosen edges from pan with a knife. Cool 1 hour longer. Refrigerate overnight.

5. Remove rim from pan. If desired top cheesecake with whipped cream and sprinkle with pistachios and crumbs.

NOTE To toast nuts, bake in a shallow pan in a 350° oven for 5-10 minutes or cook in a skillet over low heat until lightly browned, stirring occasionally.

NUTRITION FACTS 1 slice (calculated without toppings): 375 cal., 26g fat (14g sat. fat), 118mg chol., 259mg sod., 30g carb. (23g sugars, 1g fiber), 9g pro.

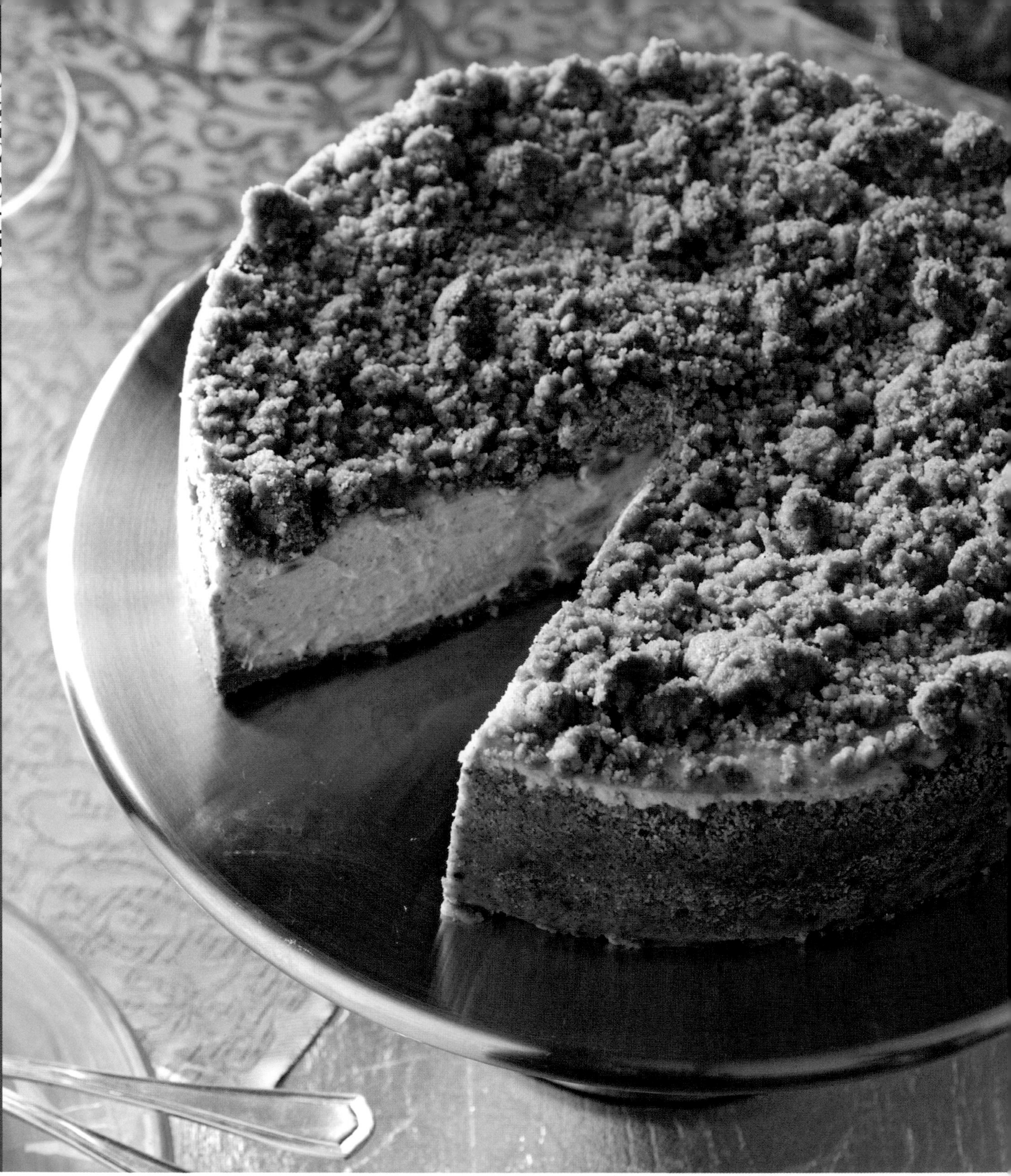

Apple Brandy Cheesecake

If you like apple pie, you're likely to love this impressive cheesecake. Bits of apple are scattered throughout the filling, and a cinnamon-brown sugar streusel makes a delightful topping.

—MARIAN PLATT SEQUIM, WA

PREP: 40 MIN. • **BAKE:** 1 HOUR + CHILLING
MAKES: 12 SERVINGS

1¼ cups graham cracker crumbs
⅓ cup ground walnuts
⅓ cup butter, melted
½ teaspoon ground cinnamon

FILLING
3 packages (8 ounces each) cream cheese, softened
¾ cup sugar
¾ cup chunky applesauce
3 tablespoons heavy whipping cream
¼ cup apple brandy or brandy
¾ teaspoon ground cinnamon
¼ teaspoon ground nutmeg
3 large eggs, lightly beaten

TOPPING
¾ cup all-purpose flour
¾ cup packed brown sugar
⅓ cup butter, melted
½ teaspoon ground cinnamon
¼ teaspoon ground nutmeg

1. Preheat oven to 350°. In a small bowl, combine the cracker crumbs, walnuts, butter and cinnamon. Press into the bottom and 1½ in. up the sides of a greased 9-in. springform pan. Place pan on a baking sheet. Bake for 10 minutes. Cool on a wire rack.

2. Beat cream cheese and sugar until smooth. Beat in applesauce, cream, brandy, cinnamon and nutmeg. Add eggs; beat on low just until combined. Pour into the crust. Return the pan to the baking sheet. Bake for 35 minutes.

3. In a small bowl, combine topping ingredients until crumbly. Carefully sprinkle over the hot cheesecake. Bake 25-30 minutes longer or until the center is just set.

4. Cool on a wire rack for 10 minutes. Carefully run a knife around the edge of the pan to loosen; cool 1 hour longer. Refrigerate overnight.

NUTRITION FACTS 1 slice: 617 cal., 42g fat (25g sat. fat), 187mg chol., 380mg sod., 50g carb. (37g sugars, 1g fiber), 10g pro.

Cherry Pudding Cake, p. 232

CHAPTER 10
SPECIAL SURPRISES
Go beyond the expected with these out-of-the ordinary baked treats!

Bread Pudding with Nutmeg

I always make this recipe for my dad on his birthday and holidays. And he always says it tastes exactly like the bread pudding with nutmeg he enjoyed as a child.

—**DONNA POWELL** MONTGOMERY CITY, MO

PREP: 15 MIN. • **BAKE:** 40 MIN.
MAKES: 6 SERVINGS

---

  2 large eggs
  2 cups scalded milk
 ¼ cup butter, cubed
 ¾ cup sugar
 ¼ teaspoon salt
  1 teaspoon ground cinnamon
 ½ teaspoon ground nutmeg
  1 teaspoon vanilla extract
4½ to 5 cups soft bread cubes
     (about 9 slices)
 ½ cup raisins, optional
VANILLA SAUCE
 ⅓ cup sugar
  2 tablespoons cornstarch
 ¼ teaspoon salt
1⅔ cups cold water
  3 tablespoons butter
  2 teaspoons vanilla extract
 ¼ teaspoon ground nutmeg

1. Preheat oven to 350°. In a large bowl, lightly beat eggs. Combine the milk and butter; add to the eggs along with sugar, spices and vanilla. Add bread cubes and the raisins if desired; stir gently.

2. Pour into a well-greased 11x7-in. baking dish. Bake for 40-45 minutes or until a knife inserted 1 in. from the edge comes out clean.

3. For sauce, combine sugar, cornstarch and salt in a saucepan. Stir in water until smooth. Bring to a boil over medium heat; cook and stir for 2 minutes or until thickened. Remove from heat. Stir in butter, vanilla and nutmeg. Serve with the warm pudding.

NUTRITION FACTS 1 piece: 419 cal., 19g fat (11g sat. fat), 118mg chol., 534mg sod., 56g carb. (40g sugars, 1g fiber), 7g pro.

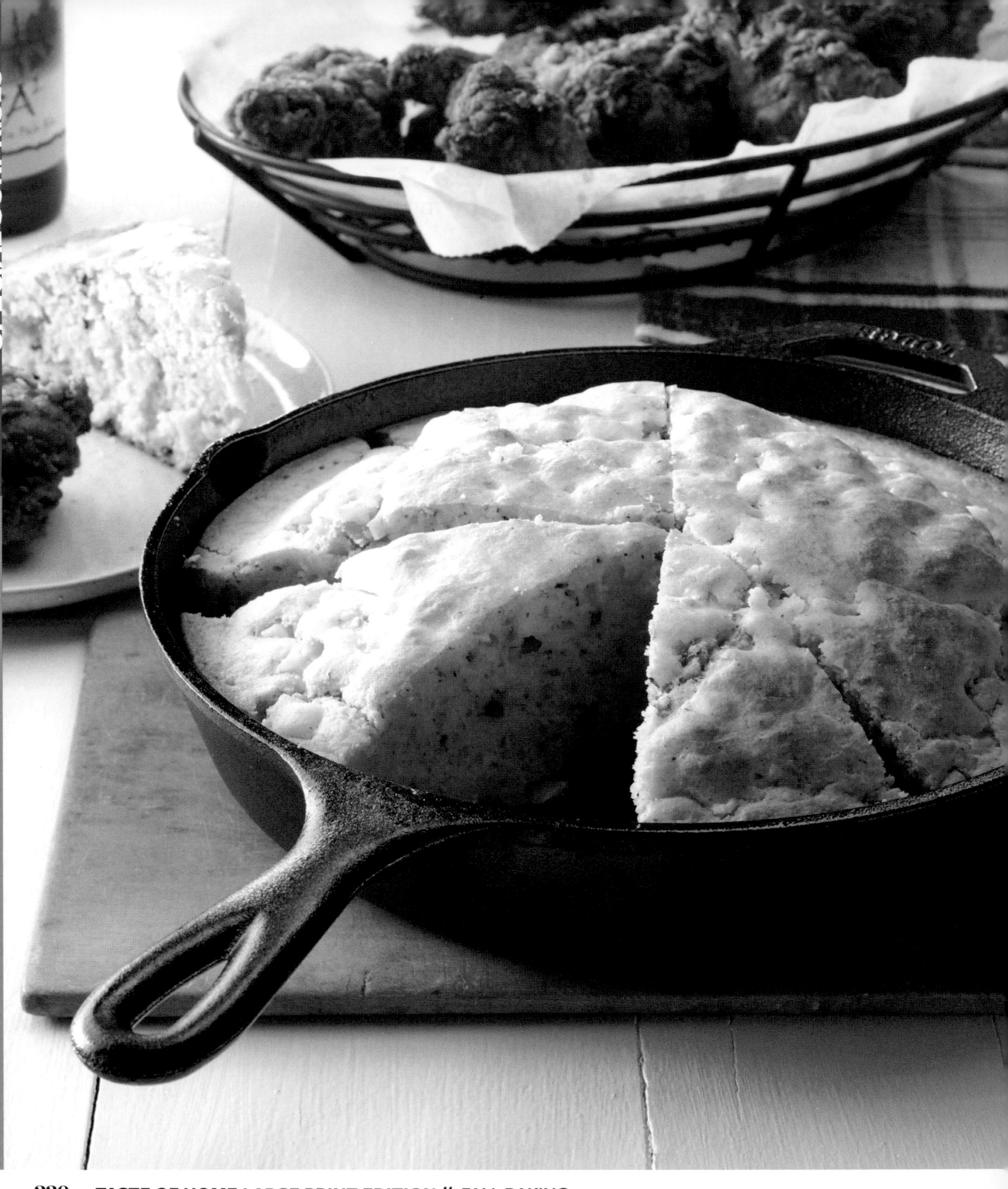

Skillet Herb Bread

My grandmother, aunts and mom were all good cooks, and each had her own specialty when it came to bread. But Mom's was my favorite—she started making it 40 years ago. The flavors call to mind the taste of corn bread stuffing!

—**SHIRLEY SMITH** YORBA LINDA, CA

PREP: 10 MIN. • **BAKE:** 35 MIN.
MAKES: 10 SERVINGS

1½   cups all-purpose flour
2   tablespoons sugar
4   teaspoons baking powder
1½   teaspoons salt
1   teaspoon rubbed sage
1   teaspoon dried thyme
1½   cups yellow cornmeal
1½   cups chopped celery
1   cup chopped onion
1   jar (2 ounces) chopped
     pimientos, drained
3   large eggs, beaten
1½   cups fat-free milk
⅓   cup vegetable oil

Preheat oven to 400°. In a large bowl, combine flour, sugar, baking powder, salt, sage and thyme. Combine cornmeal, celery, onion and pimientos; add to the dry ingredients and mix well. Add eggs, milk and oil; stir just until moistened. Pour mixture into a greased 10- or 11-in. ovenproof skillet. Bake bread for 35-45 minutes or until the bread tests done. Serve warm.

NUTRITION FACTS 1 slice: 278 cal., 10g fat (0 sat. fat), 0 chol., 595mg sod., 39g carb. (0 sugars, 0 fiber), 7g pro. *Diabetic Exchanges:* 2 starch, 2 fat, 1 vegetable.

HOW TO

SEASON A CAST-IRON SKILLET

Line the lower oven rack with foil; preheat to 350°. Scrub the skillet with hot, soapy water and a stiff brush to remove any rust. Towel-dry; apply a thin coat of vegetable oil to the entire pan, including the outside and the handle. Bake skillet upside down on the top oven rack for 1 hour. Turn the oven off; leave the skillet inside to cool.

Cherry Pudding Cake

A cross between a cake and a cobbler, this cherry dessert is awesome. Add it to your potluck recipes, because it's sure to go fast!

—**BRENDA PARKER** KALAMAZOO, MI

PREP: 10 MIN. • **BAKE:** 40 MIN.
MAKES: 12 SERVINGS

- 2 cups all-purpose flour
- 2½ cups sugar, divided
- 4 teaspoons baking powder
- 1 cup whole milk
- 2 tablespoons canola oil
- 2 cans (14½ ounces each) water-packed pitted tart red cherries, well drained
- 2 to 3 drops red food coloring, optional
- ⅛ teaspoon almond extract
  Whipped cream or ice cream, optional

1. Preheat oven to 375°. In a bowl, combine flour, 1 cup of sugar, baking powder, milk and oil; pour into a greased shallow 3-qt. baking dish. In a bowl, combine cherries, food coloring (if desired), extract and the remaining sugar; spoon over the batter.

2. Bake 40-45 minutes or until a toothpick inserted in the cake portion comes out clean. Serve warm, with whipped cream or ice cream if desired.

NUTRITION FACTS 1 serving: 296 cal., 3g fat (1g sat. fat), 3mg chol., 147mg sod., 65g carb. (48g sugars, 1g fiber), 3g pro.

Soft Giant Pretzels

My husband, friends and family love these big, soft, chewy pretzels. Let your bread machine mix the dough, then shape and bake these fun snacks.

—**SHERRY PETERSON** FORT COLLINS, CO

PREP: 20 MIN. + RISING • **BAKE:** 10 MIN.
MAKES: 8 PRETZELS

---

   1   cup plus 2 tablespoons water
        (70° to 80°)
   3   cups all-purpose flour
   3   tablespoons brown sugar
  1½   teaspoons active dry yeast
   2   quarts water
   ½   cup baking soda
        Coarse salt

1. In bread machine pan, place the first four ingredients in the order suggested by the manufacturer. Select dough setting (check after 5 minutes of mixing; add 1–2 tablespoons water or flour if needed).

2. When cycle is completed, turn the dough out onto a lightly floured surface. Divide the dough into eight balls. Roll each ball into a 20-in. rope; form each rope into a pretzel shape.

3. Preheat oven to 425°. In a large saucepan, bring water and baking soda to a boil. Drop pretzels into the boiling water, two at a time; boil for 10-15 seconds. Remove with a slotted spoon; drain on paper towels.

4. Place pretzels on greased baking sheets. Bake until golden brown, 8-10 minutes. Spritz or lightly brush with water. Sprinkle with salt.

NUTRITION FACTS 1 pretzel: 193 cal., 1g fat (0 sat. fat), 0 chol., 380mg sod., 41g carb. (5g sugars, 1g fiber), 5g pro.

Apple Dumplings with Sauce

These warm and comforting dumplings are incredible by themselves or served with ice cream. You can decorate the dumplings with leaves and stems cut from leftover dough.

—ROBIN LENDON CINCINNATI, OH

PREP: 1 HOUR + CHILLING • **BAKE:** 50 MIN.
MAKES: 8 SERVINGS

- 3 cups all-purpose flour
- 1 teaspoon salt
- 1 cup shortening
- 1/3 cup cold water
- 8 medium tart apples, peeled and cored
- 8 teaspoons butter
- 9 teaspoons cinnamon-sugar, divided

SAUCE

- 1½ cups packed brown sugar
- 1 cup water
- ½ cup butter, cubed

1. In a large bowl, combine flour and salt; cut in shortening until crumbly. Gradually add water, tossing with a fork until the dough forms a ball. Divide dough into eight portions. Cover and refrigerate at least 30 minutes or until easy to handle.

2. Preheat oven to 350°. Set each portion of dough between two lightly floured sheets of waxed paper and roll into a 7-in. square. Place an apple on each square. Place 1 teaspoon butter and 1 teaspoon cinnamon-sugar in the center of each apple.

3. Gently bring up the corners of each pastry to the center; pinch edges to seal. If desired, cut out apple leaves and stems from dough scraps; attach to dumplings with water. Place in a greased 13x9-in. baking dish. Sprinkle with the remaining cinnamon-sugar.

4. In a large saucepan, combine the sauce ingredients. Bring just to a boil, stirring until blended. Pour over the apples.

5. Bake for 50-55 minutes or until the apples are tender and the pastry is golden brown, basting occasionally with sauce. Serve warm.

NUTRITION FACTS 1 dumpling: 760 cal., 40g fat (16g sat. fat), 41mg chol., 466mg sod., 97g carb. (59g sugars, 3g fiber), 5g pro.

Dark Chocolate Croissant Bread Pudding

Croissants make an incredible base for this rich, chocolaty bread pudding. This recipe calls for semisweet, but I usually make it with dark chocolate instead. White chocolate works, too! Garnish with your favorite nuts.

—JENN TIDWELL FAIR OAKS, CA

PREP: 15 MIN. + STANDING • **BAKE:** 40 MIN.
MAKES: 15 SERVINGS

8	croissants, torn into 2-inch pieces
1	cup semisweet chocolate chunks
8	large eggs
1	cup sugar
1	tablespoon grated orange peel
1½	teaspoons ground cinnamon
¼	teaspoon ground nutmeg
⅛	teaspoon salt
3	cups 2% milk
1	cup orange juice
2	teaspoons vanilla extract

1. Preheat oven to 350°. Place croissants in a greased 13x9-in. baking dish; sprinkle with chocolate chunks. In a large bowl, whisk eggs, sugar, orange peel, cinnamon, nutmeg and salt until blended. Stir in milk, orange juice and vanilla; pour over top. Let stand about 15 minutes or until bread is softened.

2. Bake, uncovered, 40-45 minutes or until puffed and golden brown; cover loosely with foil during last 10 minutes if top browns too quickly. Serve warm.

NUTRITION FACTS 1 serving: 323 cal., 15g fat (8g sat. fat), 123mg chol., 230mg sod., 42g carb. (29g sugars, 2g fiber), 9g pro.

TOP TIP

Chocolate stays fresh for about a year if kept in a cool, dry place—dark chocolate even longer. White or gray "blooms" on the chocolate's surface means that the cocoa butter has separated. It doesn't look pretty, but the chocolate is still fine to use.

Quick Cherry Turnovers

Refrigerated crescent rolls let you make these fruit-filled pastries in a hurry. My family loves them for breakfast, but they're so delicious, they'd be welcome any time of the day. Feel free to experiment with other pie fillings, too!

—ELLEEN OBERRUETER DANBURY, IA

START TO FINISH: 20 MIN.
MAKES: 4 SERVINGS

- 1   tube (8 ounces) refrigerated crescent rolls
- 1   cup cherry pie filling
- ½   cup confectioners' sugar
- 1   to 2 tablespoons milk

1. Preheat oven to 375°. Unroll the crescent dough and separate into four rectangles; place on an ungreased baking sheet. Press perforations to seal. Place ¼ cup pie filling on one half of each rectangle. Fold the dough over the filling; pinch edges to seal. Bake 10-12 minutes or until golden.

2. Place confectioners' sugar in a small bowl; stir in enough milk to achieve a drizzling consistency. Drizzle over turnovers. Serve warm.

PER SERVING 1 turnover: 359 cal., 12g fat (3g sat. fat), 1mg chol., 459mg sod., 56g carb. (34g sugars, 0 fiber), 4g pro.

Apples & Cream Pancake

This recipe is delicious for breakfast or brunch. I usually make a double batch, because everyone wants more! With our own orchard, we have plenty of Delicious and Winesap apples—they make this a true Midwestern treat.

—RUTH SCHAFER DEFIANCE, OH

START TO FINISH: 25 MIN.
MAKES: 6 SERVINGS

½   cup milk
2   large eggs
½   cup all-purpose flour
¼   teaspoon salt
1   to 2 tablespoons butter
¼   cup packed brown sugar
3   ounces cream cheese, softened
½   cup sour cream
½   teaspoon vanilla extract
1½ cups thinly sliced unpeeled apples
¼   cup chopped walnuts

1. Preheat oven to 450°. In a small bowl, combine milk, eggs, flour and salt. Beat until smooth. Heat a cast-iron or ovenproof skillet in oven until hot. Add butter to the skillet; spread over entire bottom of the pan. Pour in batter; bake for 10 minutes or until golden brown.

2. Meanwhile, combine sugar and cream cheese. Blend in sour cream and vanilla. Fill hot pancake with ¾ cup cream cheese mixture and top with apples. Spread remaining cream cheese mixture over apples and sprinkle with nuts. Cut into wedges and serve immediately.

NUTRITION FACTS 1 piece: 265 cal., 16g fat (8g sat. fat), 108mg chol., 204mg sod., 24g carb. (14g sugars, 1g fiber), 7g pro.

DID YOU KNOW?

The saying, "An apple a day keeps the doctor away," was first used by J. T. Stinson at the 1904 St. Louis World's Fair, to market his fruit. It was derived from an English proverb: "An apple before going to bed keeps the doctor from earning his bread."

Cranberry Bread Pudding

This down-home dessert takes on a touch of elegance when I serve it drizzled with an orange custard sauce. It's so pretty that I often make it when we have dinner guests.
—**MARGERY RICHMOND** FORT COLLINS, CO

PREP: 35 MIN. + STANDING • **BAKE:** 65 MIN.
MAKES: 12 SERVINGS

- 16 slices bread, crusts removed, cubed
- 1½ cups fresh or frozen cranberries, thawed
- 1 tablespoon grated orange peel
- ¼ cup butter, melted
- 6 large eggs
- 4 cups milk
- ¾ cup plus 1 tablespoon sugar, divided
- 1 teaspoon vanilla extract

ORANGE CUSTARD SAUCE
- 3 large egg yolks
- ¼ cup sugar
- 1 cup heavy whipping cream
- 1 orange peel strip (¼ inch)
- ½ teaspoon orange extract

1. Preheat oven to 375°. In a greased 13x9-in. baking dish, layer half the bread cubes, cranberries and orange peel. Repeat layers. Drizzle with butter.

2. In a large bowl, beat the eggs, milk, ¾ cup of the sugar and the vanilla until blended; pour over the bread mixture. Let stand for 15-30 minutes. Sprinkle with the remaining sugar.

3. Bake, uncovered, for 65-75 minutes or until a knife inserted near the center comes out clean.

4. For sauce, in a small heavy saucepan, whisk egg yolks and sugar. Stir in cream and orange peel. Cook over low heat for about 15-20 minutes or until mixture is just thick enough to coat a metal spoon and a thermometer reads at least 160°, stirring constantly but gently. Do not allow to boil. Immediately transfer the sauce to a bowl.

5. Place bowl in an ice-water bath for a few minutes, stirring occasionally. Stir in extract. Discard orange peel. Refrigerate until chilled. Serve with bread pudding.

NUTRITION FACTS 1 each: 370 cal., 19g fat (10g sat. fat), 208mg chol., 299mg sod., 41g carb. (24g sugars, 1g fiber), 10g pro.

Rhubarb Popover Pie

This fabulous breakfast pie is also delicious when fresh strawberries or other berries are mixed in with the rhubarb filling. Yum!
—**PATRICIA KILE** ELIZABETHTOWN, PA

PREP: 25 MIN. • **BAKE:** 20 MIN.
MAKES: 6 SERVINGS

1/2 cup all-purpose flour
1/4 teaspoon salt
 2 large eggs
1/2 cup 2% milk
 2 tablespoons butter
FILLING
1 1/2 cups sliced fresh or frozen
      rhubarb, thawed
1/2 cup canned pineapple chunks
1/3 cup butter, cubed
1/2 cup packed brown sugar
      Whipped cream or vanilla ice
      cream, optional

1. Preheat oven to 425°. In a large bowl, combine flour and salt. In another bowl, whisk eggs and milk.

2. Place butter in an 9-in. pie plate; heat in the oven for 3-5 minutes or until the butter is melted. Meanwhile, stir the egg mixture into the dry ingredients just until moistened.

3. Carefully swirl the butter in the pan to coat the sides and bottom of pan; add batter. Bake for 16-20 minutes or until puffed and golden brown.

4. Meanwhile, in a large skillet, saute rhubarb and pineapple in butter until the rhubarb is tender. Stir in brown sugar; bring to a boil over medium heat, stirring constantly. Pour into the center of the puffed pancake; cut into six wedges. Serve immediately, with whipped cream if desired.

NOTE If using frozen rhubarb, measure rhubarb while still frozen, then thaw completely. Drain in a colander, but do not press out the liquid.

NUTRITION FACTS 1 piece: 279 cal., 16g fat (10g sat. fat), 109mg chol., 239mg sod., 31g carb. (21g sugars, 1g fiber), 4g pro.

Over-the-Top Blueberry Bread Pudding

Whether warm or at room temperature, this bread pudding truly is over the top! For a change of flavor, substitute raspberries for the blueberries.

—MARILYN HAYNES SYLACAUGA, AL

PREP: 15 MIN. + STANDING • **BAKE:** 50 MIN.
MAKES: 12 SERVINGS

3 large eggs
4 cups heavy whipping cream
2 cups sugar
3 teaspoons vanilla extract
2 cups fresh or frozen blueberries
1 package (10 to 12 ounces) white baking chips
1 loaf (1 pound) French bread, cut into 1-inch cubes

SAUCE

1 package (10 to 12 ounces) white baking chips
1 cup heavy whipping cream

1. Preheat oven to 350°. In a large bowl, combine eggs, cream, sugar and vanilla. Stir in blueberries and baking chips. Stir in bread cubes; let stand 15 minutes or until the bread is softened.

2. Transfer to a greased 13x9-in. baking dish. Bake, uncovered, 50-60 minutes or until a knife inserted in the center comes out clean. Let stand for 5 minutes before serving pudding.

3. For sauce, place the baking chips in a small bowl. In a small saucepan, bring cream just to a boil. Pour the cream over the baking chips; whisk until smooth. Serve with the bread pudding.

NUTRITION FACTS 1 each: 869 cal., 54g fat (33g sat. fat), 195mg chol., 344mg sod., 89g carb. (65g sugars, 1g fiber), 11g pro.

TOP TIP

The flavor of lavender complements blueberries extremely well. (Be sure to buy culinary lavender.) Grind the buds and mix them with the sugar, or put the buds in cream and let it stand for an hour or two. Strain the cream before making the recipe.

GENERAL RECIPE INDEX

Aunt Lou's Fresh Apple
  Cake, 203
Banana Skillet Upside-Down
  Cake, 180
Carrot Cake, 183
Cherry Pudding Cake, 232
Milk Cake, 195
Moist Chocolate Cake, 187
Moist Lemon Chiffon Cake, 192
Spiced Devil's Food Cake, 199
Walnut Pumpkin Cake Roll, 188

CARAMEL
Caramel Apple Bars, 110
Caramel-Apple Skillet
  Buckle, 161
Caramel Pecan Cheesecake, 206
Easy Mini Caramel Apple
  Cheesecakes, 209
Jumbo Caramel Banana
  Muffins, 45

CARROTS
Carrot Cake, 183

CHEESE
(also see Cream Cheese)
Apple & Cheddar Mini Scones, 41
Figgy Apple Brie Tart, 136
Khachapuri, 59
Old-World Ricotta Cheesecake, 213
Peppy Cheese Bread, 76

CHEESECAKES
Apple Brandy Cheesecake, 225

Candy Bar Cheesecake
  Brownies, 129
Caramel Pecan Cheesecake, 206
Coconut-White Chocolate
  Cheesecake, 221
Cranberry Mocha
  Cheesecake, 210
Easy Mini Caramel Apple
  Cheesecakes, 209
Lovely Lemon Cheesecake, 214
Maple-Nut Cheesecake, 218
Old-World Ricotta
  Cheesecake, 213
Pistachio Cardamom
  Cheesecake, 222
Pumpkin Cheesecake, 217

CHERRIES
Cherry Cheese Cupcakes, 196
Cherry Pudding Cake, 232
Overnight Cherry Danish, 11
Quick Cherry Turnovers, 240

CHOCOLATE & COCOA
(also see White Chocolate)
Big & Buttery Chocolate Chip
  Cookies, 95
Black-Bottom Banana Bars, 109
Boston Cream Cupcakes, 191
Candy Bar Cheesecake
  Brownies, 129
Cappuccino Cake Brownies, 106
Chocolate Chip-Cranberry
  Scones, 37
Chocolate Cobbler, 166

Chocolate Macaroon
  Cupcakes, 200
Chocolate-Peanut Butter Cup
  Cookies, 107
Chocolate Pistachio Biscotti, 88
Cinnamon Brownies, 125
Cranberry Mocha
  Cheesecake, 210
Dark Chocolate Croissant Bread
  Pudding, 239
Dark Chocolate Truffle
  Tart, 139
Fudge-Topped Brownies, 121
Moist Chocolate Cake, 187
Spiced Devil's Food Cake, 199

CINNAMON
Cinnamon Brownies, 125
Cinnamon Coffee Cake, 16
Honey Cinnamon Bars, 122

COBBLERS & CRISPS
Blueberry Buckle, 162
Blueberry Cornmeal
  Cobbler, 173
Caramel-Apple Skillet
  Buckle, 161
Chocolate Cobbler, 166
Ginger-Lime Pear Cobbler, 174
Gingersnap Rum Apple
  Crisp, 170
Macaroon Apple Cobbler, 165
Peach & Berry Bliss Cobbler, 169
Plum Good Crisp, 177
Rhubarb Mandarin Crisp, 158

ALPHABETICAL RECIPE INDEX